What Time Were You Born?

What Time Were You Born?

CREATING YOUR
COMPLETE ASTROLOGICAL CHART

SASHA FENTON

A Sterling / Zambezi Book
Sterling Publishing Co., Inc.
New York

Library of Congress Cataloging-in-Publication Data Available

2   4   6   8   10   9   7   5   3

Published in 2005 by Sterling Publishing Co., Inc.
387 Park Avenue South, New York, NY 10016
Copyright © 2005 Sasha Fenton
Published and distributed in the UK solely by
Zambezi Publishing Limited
P.O. Box 221 Plymouth,
Devon PL2 2YJ
www.zampub.com
Distributed in Canada by Sterling Publishing
℅ Canadian Manda Group, 165 Dufferin Street
Toronto, Ontario, Canada M6K 3H6
Distributed in Australia by Capricorn Link (Australia) Pty Ltd.
P.O. Box 704, Windsor, NSW 2756, Australia

Typesetting by Zambezi Publishing Ltd, Plymouth UK

Manufactured in the United States of America
All rights reserved.

For information about custom editions, special sales, premium and
corporate purchases, please contact Sterling Special Sales
Department at 800-805-5489 or specialsales@sterlingpub.com.

Zambezi ISBN-13: 978-1-903065-36-5
ISBN-10: 1-903065-36-4

Sterling ISBN-13: 978-1-4027-2272-1
ISBN-10: 1-4027-2272-9

About the Author

Sasha Fenton became a professional astrologer, palmist, and tarot card reader in 1974, but she tailed off her consultancy business once her writing career took off. Her first book was published in 1985, and she has now written more than one hundred and twenty titles, mainly on mind, body, and spirit subjects. Total sales to date are over 6.5 million copies, with translations of some titles into ten languages. Sasha now runs Zambezi Publishing Ltd. with her husband, Jan Budkowski.

Sasha wrote the stars column for *Woman's Own* magazine in Britain for many years, as well as other astrology and palmistry columns. Her articles have appeared in many newspapers and magazines in Britain and overseas. She enjoys working in radio, having broadcast on shows from Britain to Bophuthatswana and beyond. She has also had her own spot on United Artists television for five years.

Sasha's contributions to the fields of mind, body, and spirit, and writing include past service as president of the British Astrological and Psychic Society (BAPS), as a chair of the Advisory Panel on Astrological Education, and as a member of the Executive Council of the Writers' Guild of Great Britain.

Sasha has two children, Helen and Stuart, and two lovely granddaughters, Anna and Ellie.

This one is for my loving husband, Jan.

Contents

Introduction

It is interesting to see how an unexpected event can initiate an idea for a book, but being pestered by a drunken man must surely take a prize for being one of the most unusual!

This one came my way when my husband, Jan, and I decided to have lunch at a local pub as a change from eating in the office. While Jan was away at the bar ordering our food, a rather inebriated man decided that I would make the perfect audience for his ramblings. I tuned out most of his babbling until he suddenly asked me whether I had heard that people born around midnight could see ghosts and spirits. I didn't want to give him any further encouragement, so I pretended that the subject didn't interest me. He soon wandered off in search of someone else to bore.

What the inebriated man didn't realize was that he hadn't bored me at all! As an astrologer, I had long since noticed a similar phenomenon, and I knew that many people who work in the mind, body, and spirit fields are born around midnight. The drunken man drew my attention to the fact that this point must be known to others—it might even be an old wives' tale or part of local folklore.

Jan and I chatted about this over our meal. I pointed out that not only were we both born between midnight and one o'clock in the morning, but many of our friends in the mind, body, and spirit fields were as well. In fact, most of our Zambezi authors and editors were born around midnight! By the time we had finished our meal, I had the bare bones of this book sketched out in my head.

The beauty of the system that I worked out for this book is that you do not need to be an astrologer to use it, nor do you need to know the exact time of your birth. There is no need for you to even have a full birthchart drawn up. However, if you would like to have one done, you only need to check out my Web site (www.sashafenton.com) to find details of some free or low-cost Internet chart services.

Most professional astrologers are aware of the research by the statisticians Michel and Françoise Gauquelin in the 1970s. These two set out to disprove astrology...only to end up becoming renowned astrologers in their own right! They ran thousands of charts through computers and discovered that people's careers and personality types linked precisely to their time of birth.

The time of birth connects to a system in astrology that is known as the *houses*. While your Sun sign tells you a great deal about your personality, the house that the Sun was in when you were born gives much more information, and it also shows you the best way to use your natural gifts. This house position links with your time of birth, and as I said earlier in this introduction, the birth time only needs to be a rough one for you to make perfect sense of the system in this book.

1

The Basic Time Chart

The Basic Time Chart is like a twenty-four hour clock, but it shows dawn on the left-hand side, midday at the top, dusk on the right, and midnight at the bottom. The area above the horizontal line represents daytime, and the part below it represents nighttime.

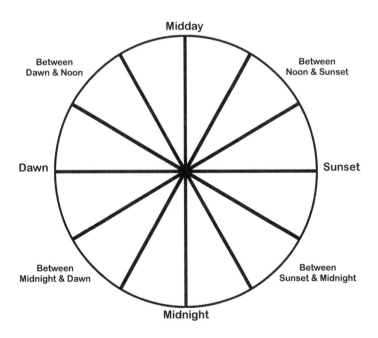

The Basic Time Chart

Using the Basic Time Chart

You might wish to make photocopies of the time chart in this book. If you cannot get to a photocopier, mark your Sun sign on the chart in the book. When drawing in the mark, use the standard astrology symbol to signify the Sun, which is a small circle with a dot inside.

QUICK TIP

If you have a fairly accurate idea of your time of birth and if you were born during daylight saving or British summer time, you must deduct one hour. However, even a fairly vague time of birth will make the system work. Later on, you may want to "rectify" your time of birth by using certain clues to work it out more accurately, which this book can help you do too.

Now read the list of eight birth times below. See which is the closest to yours and where to place your Sun symbol or your counter.

1. If you were born around dawn, put the Sun on the line on left-hand side of the chart.
2. If you were born between dawn and midday, put the Sun in the upper left-hand quadrant of the chart.
3. If you were born around midday, place the Sun on the line at the top of the chart.
4. If you were born between midday and sunset, put the Sun in the upper right-hand quadrant of the chart.
5. If you were born around sunset, put the Sun on the line on the right- hand side of the chart.
6. If you were born between sunset and midnight, put the Sun in the lower right-hand quadrant of the chart.
7. If you were born around midnight, put the Sun on the line that reaches the bottom of the chart.
8. If you were born between midnight and dawn, put the Sun in the lower left-hand quadrant of the chart.

Note: It doesn't matter whether you place the Sun symbol inside the "clock" design or outside—the choice is yours.

Two Examples

The following diagram shows the Sun's position for actor Nicholas Cage. Nicholas was born just after 5.30 A.M. The Sun was not yet up, so the Sun symbol is just below the dawn line.

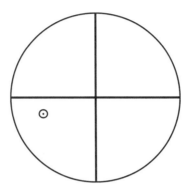

Sun Position for Nicholas Cage

Next is the Sun's position for actor Michael Douglas. Michael was born at 10:30 A.M., so his Sun is around halfway between the dawn and midday lines, in the upper left-hand quadrant.

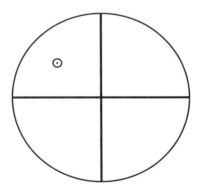

Sun Position for Michael Douglas

The Astrological Houses

The following diagram is a more complex form of the Basic Time Chart because it divides the circle into twelve segments, which correspond to the twelve houses. You will soon find yourself placing your Sun symbol in one of the houses. If you appear to fall between a couple of houses or if you are not so sure of your birth time, read the information for the house that comes before and after the one you think is right, and you will soon see which fits best.

There are twelve houses. They start at the left-hand side of the chart and they run counterclockwise.

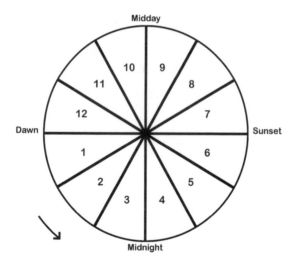

The Twelve Houses

The Elements and the Signs

Each sign belongs to one of four elements, and each element has a character of its own. Fiery people are quick, impatient, and adventurous. Earthy people are practical, but they may lack initiative. Airy people are mentally active, but they can be unrealistic. Watery people are intuitive and are led by their feelings. You will see references to these elements in the interpretation chapter.

The Elemental Groups

The fire group:	Aries, Leo, Sagittarius
The earth group:	Taurus, Virgo, Capricorn
The air group:	Gemini, Libra, Aquarius
The water group:	Cancer, Scorpio, Pisces

> **QUICK TIP**
>
> *If you decide at some point that you would like a copy of a birthchart for yourself or for one of your friends, visit one of the many astrological Web sites on the Internet. There are always some that let you draw up a chart, either for a small charge or for free. There is no need to go to the expense of buying a software program just for this purpose, unless you particularly wish to do more in-depth research. On my Web site at www.sashafenton.com, I plan to have either a free facility for this purpose or details of where you can access free natal charts on the Internet.*

Similarities

Astrology is easier than it looks. There are twelve signs of the zodiac and twelve astrological houses. It is easy to understand the houses once you know what each sign is like, since each sign links to a house. Aries is similar in nature to the first house; Taurus is similar to the second; and so on. The following table shows the connections between the signs and houses:

SIGN	HOUSE
Aries	First
Taurus	Second
Gemini	Third
Cancer	Fourth
Leo	Fifth
Virgo	Sixth
Libra	Seventh
Scorpio	Eighth
Sagittarius	Ninth
Capricorn	Tenth
Aquarius	Eleventh
Pisces	Twelfth

Two people can have different Sun signs, but if they were born at around the same time of day, they will be much more alike than one would assume at first—at least in the way that they go about their lives. The Sun sign denotes a person's character, but the house affects the way that he or she operates.

2

A Sunrise Birth

Technical Data

The dawn line in astrology represents something called the *ascendant,* also called the *rising sign.* Don't worry about this for the moment, because I will go into more detail later on.

A Birth at Sunrise

If you were born around dawn, place your Sun symbol close to the dawn line. One thing that connects most people who were born at dawn is a strong sense of self, so you can never dance to the tune of others. You learn early in life that you are an individual and that you need to do things your own way. This area of the chart breeds self-reliance and a strong survival instinct, no matter how hard life

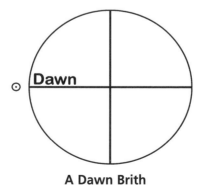

A Dawn Brith

turns out to be. The main exceptions to this rule are those of you who are born sometime after dawn, because your early life experiences can lead to a lack of confidence until you grow older and develop some inner strength. The closer you are to the dawn line, the more your Sun sign will be emphasized, which means you should be more typical of your sign. If you study astrology in more depth, you will discover that any planet (Saturn, Mercury, etc.) around this dawn line is very significant, especially when you focus on the circumstances of your childhood and youth.

A Birth Before Sunrise

If you were born before dawn, you should place your Sun symbol below the horizontal line, to show that the Sun had not yet risen. In this case, your Sun will be in the first house.

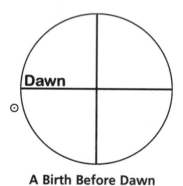

A Birth Before Dawn

Astrological theory is useful and informative, but it doesn't always fit the facts as neatly as we would like. Therefore, I suggest that if you were born at any time around sunrise—say an hour or so before or after—you read everything in this chapter to see how the different facets of a dawn birth apply to you. You may find that you are exactly like one personality type, or you may be a combination of both. Traditional astrology tells us that those born at or before dawn are extroverted, while those born after dawn are shy and apt to avoid taking risks. However, there may be areas in your life where you are tough and outgoing, and others where you are unsure of yourself and apt to hang back.

Your nature is outgoing, and it is hard for you to hide your light under a bushel. You are aware of your own needs and desires. You will always encourage your partner and your children to do well in life. You cannot sit around at home because you need your own shot at success. You have a strong will and if you have a target in sight, you will do all you can to hit it.

Other factors on your chart might exert a modifying effect, but the chances are that you are open, honest, decent, determined, and lucky. Being somewhat impetuous, you are inclined to rush in where angels fear to tread. You may be great at starting things off, seeing the wider picture, and encouraging others to get off their backsides and get going, but you find finicky details and slowly moving projects hard to cope with. Slow, fussy people will bore you. If your Sun is in an earth sign, this will be less of a problem for you, but even if your Sun sign is one of the introverted, quiet types, you will have a much sunnier, outgoing character than might otherwise be the case.

Depending on your Sun sign, you may enjoy being part of a family and having a partner and children, but you must also have an interesting career and money in your pocket. You love to travel and to shop, but you are happy to provide for yourself and your family rather than relying on others to keep you.

Some of you will gravitate to work in fashion, entertainment, or any job that is glamorous and that allows you to shine. Fire signs will seek out the limelight, but other signs may find other routes to success. This said, you are also an idealist who wants to make people happy and to make the world a better place. This combination of idealism and the desire to be known could take you into politics, trade unionism, or some other form of political leadership.

You will probably marry and have children, and you will strive to make your marriage work. However, depending on other chart factors, you might be too restless to stay with one person for long.

Either way, it is unlikely that you will be a loner. Your energy levels are high and you are highly sexed, so this can make you search around for change and excitement. This does not mean that you cannot fall in love, but once the initial excitement wears off, you get bored and start to look around again. The level of sexual restlessness will depend on your Sun sign and other factors on your chart, such as the position of your Mars.

As far as careers go, self-employment is a possibility, but you are probably happiest when working in a large organization. Whatever you do, you will want to shine. Your love of young people could take you into teaching or youth work. However, while you may drift into teaching, it may not pay well enough for you to be truly comfortable. You need a high income so that you can have a lovely home, good-quality clothes, and the opportunity to travel. Your powerful competitive streak might take you into professional sports, but even if you remain an amateur, you will always play to win.

A Birth After Dawn—Type One

If you were born shortly after dawn, your Sun symbol will be above the dawn line and in the twelfth house.

Two quite different characters can emerge from this time of birth, and much depends on your Sun sign and other features on a

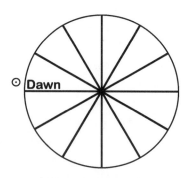

A Birth After Dawn—Type One

chart. Let us start by looking at a particular, powerful type of a sunrise personality.

Your outward manner is serious, and while you are not as outgoing (or as outrageous) as someone who was born a little before dawn, you are extremely ambitious. You have an instinct for politics, and it is a fact that many top politicians are born at this time. Three that come to mind immediately are President George W. Bush and British prime ministers Margaret Thatcher and Tony Blair, all of whom were born shortly after sunrise. The political instinct could take you to the top in a trade union, the civil service, the police force, banking, business, or some other arena that involves a good deal of politicking.

The problem is that you may become detached from reality, because if you do reach a high position, your staff and others will protect you to the point where you lose touch with the grass roots of public opinion. This is partly due to circumstances and partly due to your tendency to dream of what things should be like and then trying to impose your view onto others. Add determination, obstinacy, and bossiness and you can see how this birth time can produce a very difficult type of personality.

You may not pay a suitable amount of attention to your partner, but the weird thing is that you can be surprisingly lucky in your personal relationships despite this fact. The right partner can make up for your lack of time to spend on your children, parents, and other relatives.

A Birth After Dawn—Type Two

There is a second type of personality born at this time. This person also has the Sun in the twelfth house, but the Sun may be a little higher in the sky.

You hide your light under a bushel and you may be a "behind-the-scenes type," working quietly away from the limelight. You may concern yourself with the well-being and success of your children, family, pets and others, or you may be happy just to live a quiet life. Depending on other factors in your chart, you can become something of a martyr. The idealism of an early morning birth time is still present, but in your case, without the accompanying personal ambition. You share the desire to make the world a better place, as do the other sunrise types, but you will make your contribution in a quieter way.

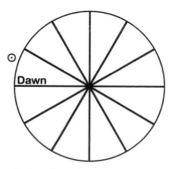

A Birth After Dawn—Type Two

You may find it hard to express yourself or even to make others aware of your true feelings, because so much of your personality hides under a shy exterior. However, the concept of self-preservation is not quite lost on you, and your heightened intuition will always come to your aid. You are quick to pick up hidden agendas and to see what is going on in the minds and hearts of others, and this allows you to stay one step ahead. You might take this natural aptitude further by becoming interested in psychology or astrology, or you might become interested in psychic, mysterious or spiritual subjects. This is especially the case if your Sun sign is in a fire or water element.

You could be an animal lover or someone who is interested in ecology, organic farming, and conservation. You are sensitive to light, noise, disturbances in the atmosphere, and tense or unpleasant people. In practical terms, it might be a good idea for you to avoid living close to electricity towers and telephone or radio antennas. In psychological terms, you should avoid living or working alongside harsh or unpleasant people. Your sensitivity might manifest itself in prophetic dreams, and you are intuitive, psychic, and "otherworldly."

Astrological theory suggests that you are likely to marry and have a family. Being far less restless than most of those born around this time, you are likely to stick things out and make marriage and family life work. Unfortunately, you may choose what you initially see as a strong partner, only to end up with a cowardly one who becomes a bully at home in order to feel powerful. You may not be able to stand your ground against a domineering partner, so it is possible that you will eventually walk away from at least one marriage in search of a gentler partner.

If you are the shy and sensitive type, the chances are that your childhood was unhappy and that your family and others did not make you feel secure or confident. Later in life, you may link up with a selfish and difficult partner, or you could sink into self-destructive behavior. It is possible for this birth time to lead a person to escape from unhappiness through drink, drugs, or other activities. It is quite possible that you will have at least one secret affair during the course of your life, possibly as part of your search for affection and understanding. This is helped by the fact that you have a knack for keeping secrets. You are kind, loving, sensitive, and sympathetic, but you may find yourself so overwhelmed by more powerful and demanding people that you eventually choose to live alone.

As far as work is concerned, you will probably choose a caring profession or perhaps one with an idealistic or humanitarian aspect. Some form of teaching or perhaps working for a charitable organization might appeal to you. You may not even be particularly interested in a structured career because you prefer to work in the world of art or music or as a psychic medium. Despite your shyness, the world of politics could still fascinate you, so you might work for your local parish, village committee, or charity. You may work on the land or with animals, in market gardening, or growing and arranging flowers. You appreciate music and beauty.

Depending on other factors in your chart, you may be interested in medical matters or alternative health and therapies, so the world of healing in all its forms may fascinate you. Tradition suggests that you are good with people's feet, so perhaps podiatry and reflexology might interest you—or maybe the "foot" connection could find you making or selling good shoes!

You must have some space for yourself, perhaps a study, your bedroom, or even a shed at the bottom of the garden, where you can retreat and where you can leave your things around and know that they will not be disturbed.

3

A Birth Midway Between Sunrise and Noon

Some Technical Points

You will need to give some thought to the actual meaning of midmorning depending on where geographically you were born, because the days are longer in the summer and shorter in the winter the farther north we go. For instance, in Canada, Norway, and other northern areas, the Sun can rise at about 2:30 A.M. in summer, so the midpoint between dawn and noon will be around 7:30 A.M. On the other hand, if you were born at a northern latitude in late December, the Sun would not have risen until around 10 A.M., so the midpoint between dawn and noon is around 11 A.M.

If you decide that you were born roughly midway between sunrise and noon, place your mark in the middle of the upper left

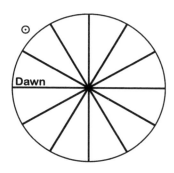

A Midmorning Birth

quadrant. When you have done this, you will see that your Sun is in the eleventh house.

If you are not sure where to put your Sun, put it in the middle of the quadrant, and then read the previous chapter, this one, and the next. You will soon see which fits you best, although some facets of your personality may fit one house division and others fit the next. For instance, you may be bold at work and wimpy in your private life, or vice versa.

A Midmorning Birth

A midmorning birth means that you have an interesting and original outlook on life. You are independent, determined, and tenacious, but your interests may not be the same as those of your friends and family. You are one of a kind. Your natural friendliness ensures that you have many close pals and many acquaintances, and some of these friends will become as important to you as your family. Some of your friends are wealthy and influential, but whether they help you realize your hopes and fulfill your wishes depends on other factors on your chart. You will certainly do a great deal for others when they are in need of your help.

The streak of idealism that surrounds all early morning births is particularly apparent here, so you might wish to spend time in work or in activities that promote the well-being of others. You may work for the benefit of animals or ecology, or in local government or some other area that is important to you. This doesn't mean that you are happy to live without material benefits, such as a nice home and high-quality possessions; it just means that these things on their own are not enough to fulfill you.

Despite your need to be in contact with people, you like to spend some time alone and to think things out for yourself. You are unlikely to choose a solitary profession, but you may be self-employed, traveling from place to place for your work. It is important for you to spend at least some time living inside your own head, reading and studying subjects that appeal to you. You are well intentioned, but demanding people can drain you, so you need to maintain a certain level of detachment. In fact, you might find it easier to get along with animals than with human beings, although you can operate well as part of a group where others take a share of the flak.

The chances are that parents and other family members expected a lot from you when you were young, and they may continue to do so throughout your life. However, this is not all one-way traffic, because you can usually count on help from family members when necessary. Your independent nature means that you can usually cope with life without asking others for help, but if you need a helping hand or a listening ear you will be able to find it. Just be careful to ensure that you live *your* life and not the one your parents want you to live. On the other hand, it is quite possible that your family will have problems and heavy obligations of their own, and in this case, your detached and independent nature will serve you well.

You have an original and inventive mind, and you are an interesting companion. Depending on your Sun sign, you should be logical and mentally attuned to problem solving. If your Sun is in an earth sign, you will be practical; if it is in a fire or air sign, you will be ingenious. A water sign adds intuition and the ability to leap to the right conclusions.

Your friendly nature ensures that you have plenty of friends and a great social life, but you also enjoy family life. A hidden lack of confidence or self-esteem might lead you into an early marriage with a partner who dominates you. If you allow a partner to run your life, your independent streak will force you to reevaluate the situation later and possibly to leave. If you are too independent for marriage, you could have several long-term relationships that are fulfilling in their way but do not tie you down.

You may choose to avoid becoming a parent, especially if your Sun is in an air sign. If you do become a parent, you will ensure that your children have a good education and all the practical help that they need. However, you will probably not be a stay-at-home parent. You have many interests, so a job or occupation outside the home is essential, especially one that allows you to teach or train others. You like to get around and enjoy a full social life. Your friendly approach means that you could do very well in sales, public relations, or perhaps some charitable area. On the other hand, your practical streak might take you into work on the land, something creative, teaching, or working in a large office. Your independent nature can also take you into self-employment in a creative or artistic field. Some of you are interested in local politics, the police or armed services, local action groups, or fund-raising for local charities. Others may develop an interest in astrology and creative lines such as design, fashion, decor, or even carpentry.

4

Late Morning to Midday

If you were born in the hours leading up to midday, you will place the mark that represents your Sun near the top of the chart but slightly to the left of the noon line.

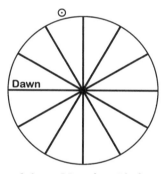

A Late Morning Birth

In theory, if you were born before midday, your Sun will be in the tenth house, and if you were born after midday, it will be in the ninth house. It is worth your while to read this chapter, the previous one, and the next one. Remember to deduct one hour if daylight saving or British summer time was in effect, as this would put your actual birth time back by an hour.

Something in your childhood taught you that life is a serious matter. Your parents may have been short of money; there may have been a number of children in the family; one child may have had special needs; or maybe some other event made life tough for you and your family at that time. This makes you cautious and determined to make the best of yourself, to earn money, to reach a position of respect, and to look after yourself and your own family later in life. In some cases, this birth time can make a person so career-minded that he or she forgets to have a private life—or a love life. Another scenario is that your parents, teachers, or others made you feel stupid, worthless, or not as clever and useful as your siblings or parents were. Either way, the result is that you strive to overcome your difficult start in life. Unfortunately, this can make you a prickly person who jumps on others at the slightest hint of criticism.

You need a meaningful career with a certain amount of status and prestige. You don't lack idealism, so you may work in a job that brings prestige and material benefits while spending some of your spare time in humanitarian or ecological occupations.

You are far more capable of coping with detailed work than those who were born earlier in the day, so this could take you into banking, accounting, publishing, or any other field where patience and an eye for detail are required. This feature will be particularly apparent if your Sun is in an earth or an air sign. The downside of this placement is that you must guard against becoming a worrywart, a moaner, or a nag.

Something in your background makes wealth, status, and position important to you. It may be that you come from a prominent family, but it is equally possible that you pulled yourself up from a lowly position. However, your innate morality means that if you are in business, you will ensure that your employees are well treated and that your shareholders receive their proper benefits. If you lose this idealism or morality in the name of achievement, your sins will come back to haunt you, and they may do so in a particularly embarrassing and public manner. Air and earth signs cannot stand being publicly embarrassed and neither can those born under the sign of Leo, so if you are among these, make sure that your heart is pure.

You do not mind working long hours or studying hard, but you may forget to have a social life or a balance between work and family life. There is always an element of sacrifice with this Sun position, especially early in life. While your friends enjoy their youth, you may stick to your college books in order to succeed. You may have fewer holidays, less time off, and less fun than others do, but you may consider the sacrifice worth it. You take responsibility easily, you are comfortable in positions of authority and decision making, and you like to others to consider you a responsible and reliable type of person. It is part of your nature to work hard, but you must take care that others do not take advantage of you. You must guard against working hard and not having your efforts recognized or working hard for too little money. The good news is that for you, life truly does begin at forty. You will not only have a long life, but the second half of it is likely to be extremely happy, and you will then learn to relax, enjoy a social life, and have a good time.

You have a strong attachment to your family. Some traditions say that the Sun in this position brings you close to your father, although my experience is that you consider all your relatives to be important to you. If you see your father as a role model, you may emulate him or even work in tandem with him. Other traditions suggest that you will be close to your children and that they will follow you into the same kind of work or lifestyle that you choose for yourself. I guess one could imagine a scenario where the whole family is engaged in a particular line of work—such as a farm, a family business, politics, or medicine.

One or both parents may lean on you or take advantage of your good nature. Alternatively, you may choose to look after your parents when they are old. Another possibility is that one parent smothers you, controls you, or tries to dictate to you. It may be hard for you to work out exactly where your boundaries are—where your parent ends and where you begin. You may have to struggle to fulfill your own dreams rather than those of your parents, your peer group, or your family as a whole. It may even take time before you know what your own dreams actually are.

Unless you were born with the Sun in the highly independent signs of Sagittarius, Leo, Aquarius, or Pisces, it is likely that your religious practices will be conventional, especially if you happen to come from a religious family. You may vaguely question their beliefs when you are young, but later you will simply fall in line and go to church, mosque, or temple on a reasonably regular basis, because you believe that is what a decent person is supposed to do. It is unlikely that you would turn your back on convention.

Fortunately, you have a lighter side, and this may take you into an interest in art, sports, dancing, amateur theatricals, playing with pets, gardening, or even astrology. You need to have fun, and you must make time for your hobbies and for friendships. This birth time suits those who collect things, such as antiques, coins, stamps, old gramophone records, and especially clocks and watches. This kind of hobby requires a head for details, a good memory, and a large shelf of reference books. Such pursuits also allow you to relax and enjoy your own company while fiddling around with your collection—and mentally assessing its growing value!

If you are not interested in a career, the competitive side of your temperament may express itself in your hobbies and social life. For instance, you may breed and show dogs, grow and exhibit flowers and vegetables, or become the top local astronomer or meteorologist.

One mixed blessing for those around you is your tendency to push your children. For instance, if you have a child who is a talented tennis player, every moment of your life will be devoted to getting him to the top of his or her game. You may run a "perfect" home and arrange wonderful dinner parties for your partner's colleagues. You may save money so that you can move to a better area and give your children better educational opportunities.

Your saving grace is your dry sense of humor. You may not show too much of this side of yourself to others at work, but when relaxing with trusted friends and with your loved ones, you really do enjoy a good laugh—and some good gossip.

Your fondness for family life means that you will find a partner and try to be happy. You are perfectly content for your partner to have an interesting career, and you will support your partner's goals. If you were born with the Sun in an earth sign or water sign, you are extremely unlikely to roam after settling down with your chosen partner. Part of this is due to shyness and lack of confidence in your own attractiveness or sexuality, but this is less likely to bother you if your Sun is in an air or fire sign. In this case, your confidence and need for independence could encourage you to play the field while young and only really settle down later in life.

It is worth noting that the Sun itself is always associated with creativity, so you may use your tenacity and ambitions in a creative way. You could create a work of art, or you could express your creativity by creating a business or by bringing up lovely children.

You may look tough and serious, but you are a real softy underneath—and your loved ones are well aware of this fact.

5

A Midday Birth

The midday line marks the boundary between the hardworking tenth house and the lucky ninth house. This point is called the midheaven in astrology—it is also known by the Latin name *medium coeli* or the initials MC. In ancient times, all astrologers and astronomers lived in the northern hemisphere, and they pointed their charts toward the Sun, which was at its highest in the sky at noon to the south. They thought this was literally the middle of the sky (medium coeli), or midheaven.

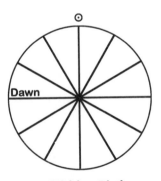

A Midday Birth

The closer you are to the noon line, the more you need to make your mark in the world. Even if you don't start out in life as an ambitious person, fate will lead you in the direction of success, status, importance, and perhaps also fame—or infamy!

You need a career that matters, that influences others, and that changes the world for the better, and this requirement may take you into a position of leadership. Your business or political instincts indicate that you will work hard and that others respect you and try to emulate you. It is quite possible that an older person will act as a mentor to you in your early days, maybe your father or some other powerful personality within your own family. While you may pursue wealth and prestige in a conventional sense, you may become known for something that doesn't involve money, such as becoming a leading eco-warrior or a Mother Teresa figure. Fame, or possibly notoriety, will enter your life at some point, and you will move among people who are famous, respected, or believed to belong to the upper classes of your area or even of your country.

Detailed work holds no fears for you, so this aptitude might take you into banking, accounting, antiques, publishing, clock and watch design, or any other field where patience and an eye for detail are required. You inspire respect in others so you seek a position of responsibility and prestige. This will be even more the case if your Sun is in an earth or fire sign.

You know that it makes sense to put money away for a rainy day. Your prudence also runs to buying quality goods and clothes that will keep their looks and value, and you take good care of the things that you buy.

Where personal relationships are concerned, you should enjoy considerable success—either as a family person or as someone who can attract many partners. You are unlikely to lose contact with your parents. If you were born with the Sun in an earth sign or water sign, family life will attract you, but you may prefer freedom to family ties if your Sun is in an air or fire sign. You may achieve status and success through a partner or relationship, but it is more likely that you will find a mentor who helps and inspires you. This relationship works well if the mentor is as loyal to you as you are to him (or her); otherwise your mentor could let you down badly. If you lose your protector or mentor, you will find another avenue and climb the ladder of success again, this time in your own right.

You prefer to keep your private life separate from your public life, so your home and family lives are sacred. Your home should be a peaceful haven where you can relax and recharge your batteries, but you must avoid taking your loved ones for granted. If you find your work exciting and your family boring, you could be in danger of losing your family. You may be a little shy when it comes to dating and sex, so you may take a while to gain the confidence to find a partner. On the other hand, you may be a very confident person who has many lovers; this birth time goes to extremes.

Most people understand that their children are unlikely to follow their example, but this concept may be hard for you to grasp. You may feel that you have worked hard to build something up and that your children should automatically take over when you retire. Although it is nice when this happens, you must not be too disappointed if it does not. All you can do is to give your children the space and the encouragement to be what they want to be. If they decide to spend their lives lying about and doing nothing, you will never be able to understand them and this will inevitably lead to a rift. However, the chances are that they will admire you and follow your example—albeit in different careers or avenues from yours.

6

A Birth Shortly After Midday

The moment that the Sun steps over the midday line, it enters the ninth house, and this house has a very different vibe from the midday or before-noon situation. However, astrology is never entirely clear-cut, because geographic and astronomical features can muddy the water. Bearing this in mind, it is worth reading this chapter and the preceding one, because you may find that some aspects of your character fit the midday or even the before-noon profile. Astrological theory states that if you were born after midday, your Sun is in the ninth house.

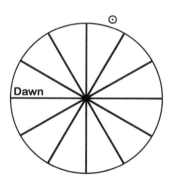

An Early Afternoon Birth

As it happens, I have just reread an old story by Somerset Maugham that demonstrates the difference between these two houses perfectly. The story concerned two brothers named George and Jim. George, the younger brother, worked hard all his life; he was a good husband and father and a respectable member of society. His hard life meant that he looked older than his years, but he comforted himself that at the end of the day, he would have a mortgage-free house, a decent pension, and the prospect of a relatively comfortable old age.

Jim was a high-living spender and a scoundrel who often borrowed money from George. Jim looked years younger than his actual age and was much more fun to be with than his hardworking younger brother was. One day, Jim overstepped the mark. He told George that someone was trying to sue him and that he might even end up in prison. George couldn't stand the thought of the family name being dragged through the mud, so he gave his rascal of a brother a large sum of money to clear the debt. Jim and the man to whom he supposedly owed the money promptly took off together to the South of France for a lovely holiday! Naturally, George gnashed his teeth and resolved never to give Jim another penny. Some time later, George heard that Jim had married an older woman who had promptly died and left him a large fortune. George almost had an apoplectic fit when he heard about Jim's luck—it was just too unfair!

This is not to say that those of you who were born after midday are happy-go-lucky rascals, but an element of luck surrounds you, so you should not have to work as hard to make a success of your life as your tenth-house cousins do. When times are hard, something always seems to come along—indeed, you may inherit money, marry money, or just be lucky in your job. This being the case, though, you don't value money for its own sake, but only for the nice things that you can buy, the freedom that it gives you, and the fun that you can have with it. Part of your luck is due to your ability to spot an opportunity when it comes along and to take advantage of it. This is particularly so if you were born with the Sun in a fire, air, or water element rather than in a hardworking earth element.

Your values are less materialistic than those of people who were born before or at midday, and your desire for status and prestige is not as obvious—although it still exists. It is possible that your chosen arena for success is spiritual rather than business-related. For instance, you may become a respected religious leader, a leading witch, or a well-loved medium and healer. One area of life that will definitely appeal to you is teaching, for which you may have a real talent. You may enjoy sports or you may keep horses as a hobby or as part of your working life. To your mind, there has to be a balance between work and your outside interests, because you believe that there is more to life than making and hanging on to money or to political power.

You enjoy being liked and admired, and you use your clever and agile mind to achieve a certain position in life, but your field of operation is likely to be an unusual one. When you try to reach a position of power and influence, however, you might fall flat on your face, because something in your nature makes it difficult for others to feel that they can trust your judgment or rely on you. This is less likely to happen if your Sun is in Capricorn, Leo, Aquarius, or Taurus. You may be a little tactless and apt to speak your mind when it would be better to remain quiet. Guard against becoming a know-it-all or talking incessantly about yourself and your own interests. On the other hand, being too humble and allowing others to make use of you is also a poor route to popularity and respect. It is sometimes hard for you to strike the right balance. The one thing that always saves you from making a complete fool of yourself and that always endears you to others is your wonderful sense of humor.

The freedom-loving aspect of your character can express itself in a variety of ways. For instance, you may take a job that allows you to move around rather than be stuck in one place. Many electricians, sales reps, and messengers belong to this time group.

You prefer going out during the evenings and weekends to sitting around at home or slumping in front of the television. Your free spirit may take you traveling, especially if your Sun is in a fire or water sign. Different cultures and places fascinate you, and this could even lead to a career in the travel industry or as a travel writer. You might live in various countries, speak a variety of languages and even marry or live with a person who comes from a completely different culture. If you take a dislike to a person, it is never because they belong to any particular race or religion. You believe in freedom of belief, free speech, and goodness to all men; you have an adventurous spirit and great good humor, along with a kind and loving heart.

The world of spirituality fascinates you, so you will wish to delve into other religions, philosophies, and ideas so that you can judge those that are worth taking up. If you grew up in a traditional or orthodox family, you will not be able to embrace your parents' views without examining them thoroughly. If you later feel that their beliefs are not right for you, you will look around for something more meaningful. You certainly read a great deal and you think deeply, so your reading will take you down many philosophical roads.

Education is your real forte because you value the acquisition and spread of knowledge. You are a good student and an excellent teacher, so if you are unsure of what career to follow, try to find something that has an element of teaching or training within it. Being energetic and athletic, you might teach some kind of sporting activity either as your main job or during your spare time. A strong desire for truth and justice means that you are outraged when you sense an injustice. In some cases, this can lead to a career in a legal field.

In personal relationships, your need for freedom can make it hard for you to settle down, or you may leave marriage until later in life. Too much responsibility worries you, and if family life becomes tough, you may reach a point where you walk away in order to preserve your sanity. You need to taste everything that the world can offer, and this will make you experimental in terms of love, relationships, and sex. However, you love children and if you have any, you are unlikely to abandon them.

7

A Midafternoon Birth

The midpoint between noon and sunset can vary greatly. For instance, in northern latitudes the sun can set as late as 10 P.M. in summer (making the midpoint 5 P.M.) or as early as 3 P.M. in winter (making the midpoint before 2 P.M.), so you have to work out for yourself whether you were born midway between noon and sunset.

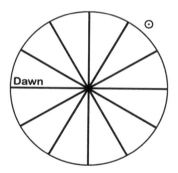

A Midafternoon Birth

If you were born midway between noon and dusk, your Sun will be in the eighth house. If you don't quite fit the description for this time group, please read the chapters that come before and after this one to see whether you fit those time groups more closely.

This birth time brings intensity to your personality and to your lifestyle. You are a deep thinker, so while you may be prepared to do a mundane job to support yourself or your family, your outside interests will be far from mundane. You are attracted to psychology and health matters and possibly also to the world of psychic and spiritual matters. This means that you could work in an area that brings healing to the minds and bodies of others.

You may tend to look back to issues in the past that have not really been resolved to your satisfaction, and it is possible that you experienced a difficult childhood. This will have left you with a cautious attitude and maybe a hidden well of resentment that surfaces from time to time. Your experiences make it easy for you to relate to suffering in others, and this itself may lead you to write an advice column or to become a social worker.

Relationships are amazingly important to you, so you probably marry or get into a permanent relationship when still young, but weak people are attracted to your strength and they may drain you or live off you in some parasitical manner. Later in life, you learn to be choosy and to pick partners who pull their fair share of the weight.

With your high energy level and powerful sex drive, you are likely to have a number of adventures, and some of these can be extremely steamy. Many charismatic actors have their Sun in this house, and they use their magnetism and sexuality to good advantage on the stage, in films, or in television. Your amazing store of energy means that you could be equally charismatic as an athlete, a dancer, an ice-skater, or in any other energetic activity that brings you before the public. It is a good idea for you to be active throughout your life, partly because it helps you to cope with your pent-up sexual energy in times of partnership famine. It is never difficult for you to attract lovers, but you can also attract and keep friends, so you will have a number of deep friendships throughout your life. Although you are happy with your own company, you prefer to be among others, to make friends, and to work in a busy environment where there are plenty of interesting people around you and lots going on.

You may not reach the top in your chosen profession, but this could be a deliberate decision on your part. You can become anything that you want, but you might prefer to work behind the scenes rather than to be the figurehead who is right in everyone's line of fire. This is especially so if your Sun is in an earth or water sign. If it is in an air or fire sign, you will be less eager to hide behind superiors or figureheads. You can keep the secrets of others, while in your personal life you can be very open in some areas and very secretive in others. This may lead you to take on a job that has a secret, confidential, or "special knowledge" content, so you may be interested in work in the armed forces, law, police force, insurance investigation, espionage, or forensic areas. Medicine also appeals to you, especially surgery and pathology.

One of the main matters indicated by this house is that of union. In business terms, this can mean that you become involved in partnerships or joint ventures, and the success or otherwise of these endeavors depends on both parties being equally honest and hardworking. Naturally, marriage or similar arrangements involve a good deal of joint ownership and blending of finances and goods, so you will make these commitments. Depending on other factors on your chart, you can be a winner or a loser in the practical and financial aspects of marriage and divorce, and there is a fair chance that you will inherit something worthwhile. At the very least, you may act as an executor for someone else's will. Death will figure in your life somewhere, although this doesn't necessarily mean that you will be bereaved; you may choose to become a bereavement counselor or you may work with the terminally ill. You may even work as a spirit medium.

The core ideas are of union and of sharing. These can signify a partnership in which the family becomes a safe and comfortable haven and creates happiness for both partners. Relationships between partners, older and younger family members, and even friends are deep, lasting, and highly affectionate. If you find the right partner, who appreciates your passion and your caring nature, you will have a wonderful marriage. This is truly the house of genuine commitment.

If you choose wrongly, you may choose a weak partner who needs to be "rescued." This type of person never really changes, so you may waste years on him or her. Alternatively, you may choose a domineering partner who makes you beg for approval, acceptance, and affection. One partner may have to bargain with the other by giving sexual favors or money for the sake of peace. One partner may play the role of servant to the other. There may be real cruelty here. Sometimes this drama plays out between a parent and child. One person can try to control what the other eats, drinks, smokes, and perhaps what they read, watch on television, and much more. One thing for certain is that control will be an issue somewhere in your life.

This is a house of secrets, so your main relationship may not exist within the family. Indeed, you may enjoy a longstanding secret affair—or even a number of them. You may decide to stay with your main partner for financial reasons. Whether in business or in your private life, the financial side of things makes it hard for you to turn your back and walk out when you should.

In family relationships, money and possessions may be shared equitably, with everyone being content—or they may be used as weapons. Consider the wealthy parent who threatens to cut the adult child out of his or her will if the child doesn't do what the old tyrant wants. You may enjoy successful business partnerships, but you could just as easily find yourself working for a rapacious manager who uses and swindles others. There may be a longstanding legal battle or struggles over business, property, children, divorce, money, and possessions.

You may have a happy life at home and at work but suffer problems relating to fertility and childbearing. This area of the horoscope is concerned with birth and death; therefore, circumstances surrounding these issues can figure in your life in any one of a hundred different ways. There may be police investigations, legal matters, or skeletons in the closet, and you may even have to leave your country of birth due to war or some political factor.

Doctors, hospitals, surgeons and surgery, investigations, and medicine may figure in your life. This is fine if you are interested in complementary therapies or spiritual healing, but you may have to spend some time in a hospital yourself. The mysterious aspect of this house might take you into psychic investigation, mediumship, or Wicca.

The main drawback to having the Sun in the eighth house is that you may spend too much time living in the past. On one hand, you may view your past as a golden age, but on the other hand, you may carry past resentments around for far too long. It is hard for you to live in the here and now. You find it difficult to forgive those who have hurt you and you may wish that you had stood up to them in a more positive manner.

There is a private side to you, and this means that you need a room or some space of your own, where you can keep things and know that they will not be disturbed. This may be a study, your bedroom, an attic room, or even a garden shed. You need to hide away from time to time so that you can think deeply and dream a little without other people bothering you.

Despite your serious attitude to life, you have a wonderful sense of the ridiculous and a terrific sense of humor. This endears others to you and saves you from falling into depression or taking yourself too seriously at times. You will love deeply and probably be loved deeply by others in return.

8

A Birth Before Sunset

If you were born in the hours just before sunset, you must put your Sun sign mark a little above the line on the right-hand side of the chart. This will place your Sun in the seventh house. However, there are various reasons why you may not quite fit, so it is worth reading this chapter, along with the one that precedes it and the one that follows.

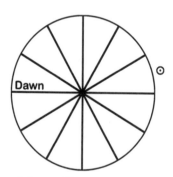

A Late Afternoon Birth

In days gone by, this was called the house of marriage, but it is now known as the house of open relationships. This includes any kind of relationship—which may be personal, business, or anything else where you are closely involved with one or more people. While the previous (eighth) house refers to the financial side of partnership and sharing resources, goods, land, mortgages, and even debts, the seventh has more to do with how you get along with others on a social or emotional level. It can lead to ideal love relationships, dreadful ones, and important business connections.

You may work in a large or small organization, but it is important for you to like your colleagues and to be happy in your work. The seventh house rules cooperation, convincing others, compromise, and mild competition. On a less pleasant note, this house also rules open enemies and warfare.

If your Sun is in the seventh house, you seek harmony, social grace, refinement, social acceptability, and pleasantness. On the other hand, you can sometimes put your foot in your mouth and you might be argumentative. Sometimes you spoil your relationships by behaving childishly or in some socially unacceptable manner, but usually only when you are sick, unhappy, or perhaps drunk! You hate to feel that you don't measure up in social situations, so you seek to rectify your mistakes—or forget about them as soon as you can. You will hate censure and ridicule if you were born under the fixed signs of Taurus, Leo, Scorpio, or Aquarius.

You appreciate beauty in all its forms and you have good eye for form and color, but your greatest love is music. You may have a good singing voice or play a musical instrument. You may be a wonderful dress designer or architect, but you can excel in any career that encompasses an element of design. There are so many career options that could be mentioned here, including gardener, chef, makeup artist, or hairdresser. You can make anyone look good and you probably look pretty good yourself, because this house tends to be filled with nice-looking people. You have great style, so your home and your place of work will be attractive and stylish. Rough, uncouth people upset you, so you seek out those who are refined, pleasant, and intelligent, but self-important people who have no real substance do not impress you. Your pleasant, friendly attitude ensures that you are never at a loss for company, although you do appreciate having some time to yourself, especially if you were born under the signs of Taurus, Leo, Libra, or Capricorn.

You cannot go through life without love, and you will choose partners who are as stylish, attractive, and interesting as you are.

Despite the fact that this house is so closely concerned with partnerships, you also require a measure of freedom and independence. You may start a career or your romantic life in a partnership, but you could just as easily leave and go it alone for a while, perhaps forming different partnerships later on. You might marry young and stay in the relationship, but only if you are not kept on a leash. You tend to bicker when you are sick or downhearted, so your partner must be able to cope with this. In a way, you are better at dating than you are at mating. One thing for sure is that your strong sex drive and loving nature mean that you will not want to be alone for long.

You have a strong sense of justice and you hate to see unfairness or bad behavior in others. Along with your ability to argue both sides of a case, this can take you into the legal profession or into work as an arbitrator or negotiator. You will always strive to enhance and improve things for yourself and for others.

9

A Sunset Birth

If you were born when the Sun was actually setting, your Sun sign will be right on the dusk line.

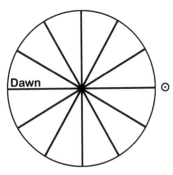

A Sunset Birth

The situation here is similar to that in the previous chapter, but there might be some added factors. You link easily with others and you work well as part of a team. You make friends easily and you try to enjoy life as much as possible. You live in the present rather than by brooding on the past, and you have an optimistic outlook on life. You are tougher than you look, so while you don't look for arguments (most of the time) you can certainly stand up for yourself when the need arises. Your balanced mind makes it hard for you to come to a decision, as you tend to see both sides of an argument. However, once you have made up your mind, it takes the equivalent of a nuclear explosion to make you change it.

One downside is that you may spend too much time and energy arguing about silly things rather than concentrating on the larger picture. It may be hard for you to assess your own worth, because you tend to measure yourself by the opinions of others. That is fine if you are among people who validate you and who tell you that you are special, but it is not so good if you surround yourself with critical or emotionally destructive people. Another problem is that legal disputes can go on too long and become emotionally and financially draining.

Others may try to live through you, or you may try to live through others. This might lead to an old-fashioned kind of marriage where the husband is a captain of industry and the wife keeps a nice house and entertains well. Another possibility is that a partner of either sex is a glamorous and successful figure in the arts, athletics, the theater, pop or classical music, or some other area, and you act as the support system, or vice versa. These scenarios may be unfashionable today, but they may work well for you, especially when each partner makes a necessary contribution to the relationship. As long as there is love and plenty of loving sex, you will probably be very happy with almost any arrangement.

Note: It is worth reading the previous and following chapters to see whether your personality fits those time profiles as well.

10

A Birth Just After Sunset

If you were born shortly after the Sun set, you need to put your Sun marker just below the dusk line, which is on the right-hand side of the chart. This puts your Sun in the sixth house.

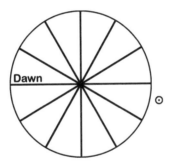

An Early Evening Birth

Unfortunately, astrology doesn't always fit our lives as neatly as we would like it to, so some parts of your nature or behavior may be closer to those of a person with the Sun in the seventh house. If you were born a little later in the evening, you could have certain characteristics that are more like those of a person whose Sun is in the fifth house. Therefore, I suggest that you read this chapter and then those that come before and after it.

This birth time is associated with two quite clear-cut concepts: work and health. This Sun placement is not likely to make you less healthy than anyone else, but it can make you very conscious of health matters. At worst, this can encourage you to become a hypochondriac and a worrier who bores everyone else to death with your neuroses, but in most cases, this house placement leads to a realistic interest in health matters. Understandably, this can lead you into a career in some area of health, healing, or the fitness industry. This placement might lead you to sell health products, to teach yoga, or to work in a gym, as a swimming instructor, or perhaps as a hypnotherapist or a Reiki healer. As you can see, there are many applications for a career or spare-time activities. You may be interested in mental health, psychology, and astrology (owing to its connection with psychology). The downside to your interest in health and nutrition is that it adds fussiness to an already fussy nature. You may make a huge issue over the kind of food that you are prepared to eat. This is fair enough if you are the one who does the shopping and cooking, but it is not so easy on those who have to cater to your wishes. If you force your eating pattern on the entire family, life in your household can be extremely grim.

Although we call this the house of work, the old-fashioned term is "the house of servants and masters." Above all, this house symbolizes duty. Your job or daily tasks may be important to you, and you may only feel happy when doing something useful. You may be one of those people who enjoy doing a pile of ironing, because you end up looking happily at the folded pile of nice clean clothes and enjoying the feeling of a job well done. As this birth time also denotes your attitude to employees, it is probable that you will find yourself in charge of others in the position of a supervisor.

You enjoy mundane tasks such as sewing, gardening, decorating, cooking, or craft work, and you may have quite an artistic eye. Whatever you do, whether it is part of your job or a sideline, you do it to the best of your ability. Your standards are high and you do not like to let others down, so you can be relied on when the chips are down.

You might be the linchpin for the family, caring for sick or needy relatives or in charge of an extended family. There is often a measure of sacrifice here, so you may find yourself giving up your freedom or your chances for personal fulfillment and happiness on behalf of family members or others. At worst, you can be a sap, used and abused by others, so you must ensure that you are not surrounded by freeloaders.

Some of those who have the Sun in the sixth house take on the role of rescuer. You may attach yourself to those who are alcoholic, drug-dependent, debt-ridden, irresponsible, and unwilling to respect themselves or others, and you may work yourself into the ground for them. Alternatively, you may help others who have lost out in life by no fault of their own. One way of serving others in a positive manner is by becoming a scout leader or youth worker or by working with the elderly, handicapped, animals, or with others who need help. Naturally, you need appreciation, acceptance, and respect for what you do, and it is nice if you get it. If you do not, then you must reassess your situation before you become angry and resentful.

You can be critical and prickly, but you are also extremely hard on yourself. You may criticize others but you also criticize yourself. You are well meaning, but your critical nature can make you difficult to live with. Be sure that, while being of service to others, you don't make them pay for it by having to put up with sharp, critical remarks.

You have an eye for detail and you can cope with secretarial or analytical work. Sloppy or disorganized people get you down, especially if you happen to be a Taurus or a Leo. You work hard at what you do and you are a perfectionist, but you cannot expect others to be the same. Oddly enough, you may not be the tidiest person in town, but you know where everything is and you resent it when others interfere with your paperwork, your office, your kitchen, or any other base of operations.

11

A Birth Between Sunset and Midnight

The midway point between sunset and midnight can vary greatly. In northern latitudes, the Sun can set in the early afternoon in winter and late at night in summer, so you will have to work out for yourself where the middle area lies.

In theory, if your Sun lies somewhere between dusk and midnight, it will be in the fifth house, but the time of day and astrological house don't always match up as neatly as we would like. I suggest that you cover all the bases by reading this chapter and those that come before and after it.

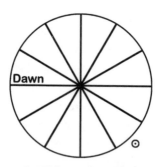

A Midevening Birth

If your Sun is in this position, you have an attractive personality, you probably look very good, and you definitely want others to love and admire you. This is no bad thing, because it makes you behave in a way that makes you lovable. In some cases, this pleasant attitude is purely superficial and can hide selfishness and childishness, but often it is genuine. You need to feel valued. This urge may be the result of your childhood experiences, but it may just be an intrinsic part of your nature. If your parents wanted you and loved you, and you made them proud and happy, you will want others to view you in the same light. On the other hand, if your parents, teachers, and peer group didn't think much of you when you were young, you will go all out to make sure that others admire you in adulthood. Either way, you court the friendship and good opinion of others.

You may find it hard to love yourself and you may need to learn to value yourself, or alternatively, you may become very pleased with yourself, which leads to an unpleasantly opinionated or pompous attitude. Your sense of humor and your intelligence will probably save you from becoming a complete pain or a laughingstock. You cannot stand it when others laugh at you, and this prevents you from becoming boastful or silly.

You need romance, love, fun, and a deeply loving connection with other people. It is possible that you rush around looking for this in a series of love affairs, but you could just as easily be content with a rich and loving family life. The latter has considerable charms as far as you are concerned, because it means that you should have children, and nobody loves children more than you do. You make a wonderful parent because you are deeply loving, understanding, and kind, but you won't spoil your children or stand any nonsense from them. You give your children love, attention, and the best education possible, but you won't allow them to be offensive, greedy, or selfish. They know exactly where the boundaries lie.

Your love of admiration makes you reach for the top, so depending on your chosen sphere of excellence, you may become an entrepreneur, captain of industry, politician, major artist, musician, or sports star. You will certainly shine in your chosen profession. Many show business personalities, movie stars, pop singers, and musicians have the Sun in the fifth house, just as many top salespeople do. Even if you don't reach these dizzying heights, you will count for something in your circle and within your family. Others will see you as a decent and honorable person. You don't wish to let others down, so you will always try to do your best.

This house is particularly associated with fun, leisure, and pleasure, so while you are prepared to work hard, you definitely need time off to play and to enjoy life. Your hobbies and spare-time activities could include almost anything, but holidays, changes of scene, and sports or games that bring you pleasure are likely to be part of the package. You like comfort and luxury, so you will not appreciate hiking over stony hills in cold, wet weather or sleeping in a tent and doing your laundry in a bucket halfway up Mount Everest. You cannot stand discomfort if you happen to be a Taurus, Gemini, Leo, or Libra. If you are an Aries, Sagittarius, or Pisces, the need for luxury is less apparent and you can put up with a certain amount of discomfort and even hardship and still imagine that you are having fun.

Depending on other factors in your chart, you may chase after romantic love and have one love affair after another. That first heady feeling that anything can happen makes you feel alive. This can lead to an interesting life…albeit an unsettled one.

You have style, class, and looks. Even if you are not conventionally good-looking, you make the best of what you have, and you always manage to appear glamorous and fascinating. The clothing, perfume, and cosmetics departments of good stores are your spiritual home, and you spend your spare time punishing yourself in the gym so that you can maintain a good figure or physique. You can let yourself go at times, either when you're depressed or when you want to relax and take a break, but before long, you will be back at the beauty parlor or hovering around the clothing racks to bring yourself back up to scratch once again. You can even manage to look good without spending a fortune— especially if you were born under an earth or water sign. Mind you, Scorpio can be the exception here, because Scorpios can spend wildly on just about anything when the mood hits them. Air and fire sign people are convinced that some good fairy will come along and wave a magic wand over their credit cards and bank overdraft, making them disappear.

Your creative nature can take you into music, fashion, decor, and design, but it can also refer to the creation of a business, making a wonderful garden, or bringing any kind of idea or enterprise to life. There are many forms of creativity, but one is the creation and love of children, so this is likely to be an important area of your life. Children also allow you to behave in a childlike manner, to play and be silly at times—and it is important for you to do this. If you do not have children, you may pour your affection on animals and pets.

This is the house of ego, pride, high standards, and a certain amount of competitiveness. This is fine in its way, but you should avoid turning your marriage or partnership into a contest. An odd little incident stands out in my mind that illustrates this point: I was at someone's party—the kind of party where people sit around eating something from paper plates perched on their laps and talking to one another. A young couple sat opposite me and bickered nonstop throughout the meal. She was a nurse and he was a teacher; neither was well paid, and the couple struggled to bring up their children while they both worked. They spent the evening arguing about the relative importance of their jobs to the community, and whether a teacher was more important to society than a nurse and vice versa. If I could have found somewhere else to sit, I would have done so.

Older forms of astrology link this house to the father or to father figures. One hopes that your father is worthy of your love and respect, but even if he is not, his influence will be a powerful one. If your father gave you approval, acceptance, and validation, you will be a well-adjusted adult. If this was not the case, you may spend your life striving to please him—even long after he is dead and gone.

12

A Birth Shortly Before Midnight

For this birth time, you must put your Sun at the bottom of the chart, fairly close to the midnight line, but to the right side of it.

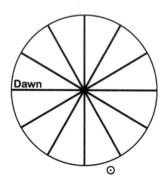

A Late Evening Birth

Astrology is not always as cut-and-dried as we would like it to be, so while your Sun should be in the fourth house, this profile may not quite fit. Even when the time of birth is on the birth certificate, you may actually have been born a little earlier or later than you think, and if you were born when daylight saving or British summer time were in operation, you may even have actually been born the day before your birthday—if you see what I mean. I know this situation very well, because it happened to me. I was born at 12:52 A.M., but British summer time was in operation and the clocks had been put forward by one hour. Therefore, my universal time at birth was actually 11:52 P.M. on the previous evening. If you have any doubts about your birth time, read this chapter, the one before it, and the two that follow it as well.

A birth before midnight should put the Sun in the fourth house. This house is closely associated with the family and with family matters, so there is usually a powerful link to at least one parent—usually the mother.

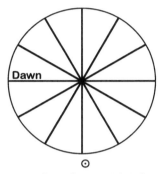

A Birth Before Midnight

While one hopes the relationship between you and your mother is a wonderful one, it may not be so. What does seem to be clear is that a mother and mother figures in general exert a powerful influence. For example, your mother may be warm, loving, caring, understanding, and in every way a helpful, comforting, and validating influence on you. Alternatively, she could be someone who stands up to adversity, makes something of herself, and therefore becomes a wonderful role model. Even if your mother is truly dreadful, her influence will be hard to shake off.

Common scenarios are those of a father who leaves and loses contact with the family, or one who dies. Either way, this means that your mother has to raise her children alone. Sometimes the father is around but not interested in you, or he makes himself unavailable to you. I have come across scenarios where the father was sick, alcoholic, or busy traveling a great deal. Whatever the truth of the matter, your mother and other female figures will play a major role in your life. It is interesting to note that, in this case, the mother often lives to a great age, so she is likely to be part of your life for many years. It is possible for the powerful parent figure to be the father or some other person, but the pervading influence is usually female.

The traditions, beliefs, value systems, and priorities that were important to your mother and to the family permeate your consciousness. This may encourage you to follow in the family footsteps or, alternatively, to reject the family's values and to find your own belief system. It is possible that you were born into a dynastic family where certain attitudes and expectations prevail. In a case like this, marriage and other unions can be matters of politics, finance, or dynasty rather than primarily of attraction or love.

In practical terms, the fourth house also refers to the household—in particular, the kitchen, fridge, stove, and cooking implements. As the Chinese would have it, the fourth house rules the heart and soul of the household. In governmental terms, it is connected to the provision of food and essential services to the population. This can lead to a career associated with the provision of food or other necessities, but it can just as easily indicate working from home. You may start some kind of business at home (not necessarily food-related) and then branch out later into other premises—probably close to where you live.

You certainly need a base of operations, and you cannot live out of a suitcase or squat in other people's houses. You need your own home, your own space, and often a room of your own; you may even keep it locked so that other family members cannot get into it. If you have a child who likes to retreat to his or her own room, consider whether his or her Sun is in the fourth (or possibly the eighth or twelfth) house. You need to escape from other people from time to time and to have your own private space. You may have a study, a bedroom, or even a garden shed, where you keep your things and where you can hide away and work or meditate.

Real estate is an important feature in your life, so you will move heaven and earth to acquire a home of your own. You may inherit a property or you may sell an inherited property and then use the money to buy your own house. In some cases, the property in question is a shop or a workshop of some kind. Even if you rent your property, you will make it your own. You may be so interested in property that you work as a real estate agent or a property developer. You will probably choose to work in a field that brings benefits to the public, and your work could bring you into contact with the public on a regular basis. An obvious option is for you to run a small shop, but you might work in insurance, banking, or some other field that brings you close to people.

You feel a strong link to the past, so family heritage or family history can be important, and there may be a kind of collective family memory that has a strange effect on your life. Sometimes there are religious factors or an aristocratic or dynastic background; sometimes there is just a family feeling and a fondness for the places and people that are associated with the past.

Your greatest problem is that you are extremely sensitive, vulnerable, and easily hurt, but you also have a greater capacity for joy and happiness than many others do. Your memory is good and you forget very little, so you never forget those who have hurt you or those who have helped you. This makes you cautious when it comes to dealing with people whom you don't know well, and it takes time for you to relax and trust others. Your sensitivity makes you intuitive and probably also psychic. I discuss this side of things more deeply in the next chapter, so it is worth reading that now.

13

A Midnight Birth

This birth time puts the Sun at the bottom of the chart on the midnight line.

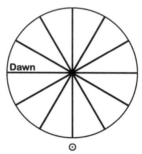

A Midnight Birth

It would be unusual for a person to be born exactly at midnight, so if you are not quite sure whether you were born a little before or a little after this time, read the previous and following chapters in addition to this one.

This chapter leads us back to the strange event that encouraged me to write this book in the first place. You may remember from the introduction that a drunken man in the pub set this project off by saying, "It is well known that people born around midnight can see ghosts and spirits." Well, whether people born around midnight are routinely haunted or not, I have long since been aware that many of those born around midnight are psychically gifted. Many become so interested in various facets of the mind, body, and spirit world that they end up working in it as healers, astrologers, Tarot readers, mediums, psychic artists, palmists, dream interpreters, and so on.

Jan and I met through our mutual interest in astrology, and we both entered the world shortly after midnight, as did most of the authors who write for Zambezi Publishing. In fact, we joke that this birth time is a prerequisite for writing our mind, body, and spirit books! It is interesting that our midnight writers include three practicing witches in addition to an astrologer who has looked deeply into the subject of witchcraft. Perhaps the "witching hour" not only affects things that happen, but the nature of children born at that time. Among our non-witch midnight writers, we have Tarot readers, astrologers, healers, crystal gazers, and many others of the kind. It is interesting that all this used to be called "occult"—which meant *hidden*—because at midnight, the Sun is on the other side of the Earth and, therefore, *hidden*.

This area of the chart is associated with one's private life: the home, family, and parents—especially the mother. Your family may be wonderful and a real blessing to you, but it is equally possible that your family is a complete pain in the neck and a real trial to you. Either way, the family connection will be strong and enduring. It seems that the connection to the family (especially the female side of it) is also a factor regarding psychism, because many psychics seem to inherit their tendencies from a mother, grandmother, or some other female relative.

It is probable that your childhood was difficult, and your family may have had an awful struggle that has gone down in family history. Intuition and psychism are a survival mechanism, so your own personal background within your family is probably at work here.

You are extremely sensitive, so critical remarks can damage you, and you never forget those who have hurt you. By the same token, you are so loyal that you often stand by those who hurt you. Your good memory works in practical ways too, so you may rely on it in your job. Perhaps you are the family's "encyclopedia" to whom everyone turns when they want to know something. This is especially so if what they want to know concerns the family's heritage and history.

Your excellent memory works in practical ways too, so you may rely on it in your job or you may be the one that your children turn to when they want to know about their family and background.

14

A Birth in the Early Hours

If you were born some time after midnight, you need to put the symbol for your Sun to the left of the midnight line.

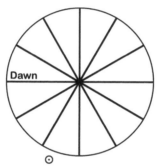

A Very Early Morning Birth

Astrology doesn't always work perfectly, as it can be affected by daylight saving time, British summer time, and an error in the time of birth, among other things. Read this chapter, the two that precede it, and the one that follows just to make sure, because you may find that you have characteristics that are common to more than one house.

Like the fourth house, the third house has robust family connections, especially with siblings. A sibling can be a brother or sister, and this link is likely to be with brothers, sisters, and others of your generation who are close to you. In some instances, you can be closely involved with a cousin, a lifelong friend, or a neighbor. These people will figure in your life in some important way, and the situation can be truly lovely, really awful—or both at various times.

Looking back to the days when I worked as a consultant astrologer, I remember a client who had a bunch of planets, including the Sun, in the third house. These planets showed that this house was stressful in some way. I suggested to the client that her siblings either had problems themselves or had caused problems for her. She replied that she loved her two siblings dearly but that they were both mentally and physically handicapped and that her parents' time and energy had been absorbed by their needs, leaving little time for my client. This is an unusual case, but it shows what can happen. However, the Sun is a happy planet, so the chances are that your sibling relationships are happy ones.

You might become closely involved in the lives of your neighbors or with events connected to your community. In our area, there is a small community hall where people run day care centers and drop-in centers and give training in basic computer work and so on. If I were to look at the horoscopes of those who give their time to this center, I bet I would find strong third-house connections.

Local travel used to mean getting around one's village, but these days it can mean much more. If you regularly travel across the country on business or have important connections in some other area—even overseas—this can be viewed a third-house matter nowadays. Vehicles and the mode of transport that you use might be an important feature in your life, so you may commute a fair distance to your work or you may have a large range, farm, or sheep ranch to get around. As you can see, local matters can denote distances of many miles these days.

If you were born with the Sun in this position, you are definitely not a loner. Your written and verbal communication skills are excellent, and you might use these in your job or just as part of your life. You might work in journalism or broadcasting, as a travel agent, or in some other job that involves passing information on from one group of people to the next. You need companionship and company, so your social life will be full and interesting. It is quite possible that you move in influential circles and have many prestigious or respected friends. You may work on a committee or become involved in a cause. This is especially so if your Sun is in a fire sign or the air sign of Aquarius.

The one thing that drives you crazy is boredom and repetition. You need a stable home life, but your work must include a variety of different tasks during the course of each day. You are quick and clever and you can think on your feet, so you get jobs done with great efficiency, often handling several tasks at the same time. You enjoy a good laugh and a good time, but you are not silly or frivolous: you take your responsibilities seriously, but you do need to strike a balance and play as well as work. Your natural aptitude for working with numbers and words and working with your hands can lead you into many different careers or pastimes, so there are plenty of career options for you to choose from.

There is no reason to suppose that your love life and personal relationships are particularly difficult. You need some time and space for yourself, and you give your partner room to maneuver as well, as long as he or she is true to you. Friendship is as important to you as love, so your partner must be someone with whom you can chat at the end of each day and whose company you relish when on vacation, playing games as a couple, or with the family as a whole.

Looking good and feeling good are important to you, so you take care of your health, your body, and your appearance. You may be tempted to spend too much money on clothes and accessories such as bags and scarves at times, but as long as you don't keep on overdoing things, it will simply serve to brighten up your life. You may not be too devoted to housework, but you need your home to look tidy and pleasant, so you may employ someone to do this for you. Males with the Sun in this house love cars, radio, and musical equipment and gadgets.

15

A Birth Between Midnight and Sunrise

If you were born in the early hours of the morning but well before sunrise, you must put your Sun symbol in the middle of the lower

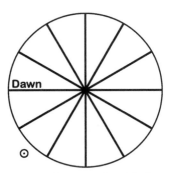

An Early Morning Birth

left-hand quadrant of the time chart. This puts your Sun in the second house.

It is highly unlikely that you are irresponsible, stupid, or wasteful, because this house placement endows you with common sense and practicality. You need to be in charge of your own money and to have a home and all the normal material comforts—and you avoid getting into debt. Yours is the sign that uses only credit cards sparingly and pays the balance at the end of each month. It is impossible for you to live without something set aside for a rainy day. It may well rain at times, but you will soon look around for work—even a second job if necessary—and you will get your finances back on track in the shortest time possible. You aren't especially money-minded or materialistic; you just need to feel secure. This said, you must guard against your natural caution turning into materialism and even miserliness—especially if you happen to have been born under an earth sign.

I have come across some people with this placement who are not motivated when it comes to work, but even they will look for a job when the money starts to run out, and all second-house people have a strong survival instinct. Some also are always looking for their big break. This is more likely to be the case with an Aries, Libra, or Sagittarius, as they are often able to live by their wits rather than by hard work.

You cannot live in uncomfortable surroundings and you will do your best to make your home beautiful. Indeed, it may be too clean and tidy for comfort, and you may find it hard to cope with the mess that children or animals cause. In fact, you may be so uncomfortable at the thought of sharing your space with children that you decide against having them.

As far as your career is concerned, you might choose to work in a practical field, such as building houses, landscape gardening, or engineering. This kind of work tends to be a good money maker and it often includes overtime at extra pay, so that would suit you admirably. You are less suited to self-employment than you are to a regular job and a regular wage. Some of you find work in the finance industry or as accountants, where your competence with details and a natural affinity for working with numbers come to your aid. Computers do not hold any fears for you either.

On the other hand, the world of music might appeal to you, and if you happen to be a Taurus, Leo, Libra, or Scorpio, you may sing or play an instrument professionally or as a sideline. The world of show business has a mild attraction for you, and if you are a Taurus, Leo, Virgo, Libra, or Pisces, you could find yourself on the stage. You may choose to become a behind-the-scenes operator in the entertainment industry by recording music, working on photo shoots, in a makeup department, or as a theatrical dressmaker or wardrobe minder.

Your senses are strong, so this can lead to an interest in things that look and taste good. Cooking and gardening appeal to you, and you like to grow the fruit and vegetables that you cook. In a practical sense, there isn't much you can't handle, so it would be unusual for you not to have a career or a hobby that allows you to use your creativity—not to mention using your hands, your five senses and your common sense.

Where love is concerned, you go to extremes, but you are certainly happiest in a solid and lasting relationship. You might be the kind of partner who goes to great lengths to make your lover happy. However, even among the best of you, there is a selfish streak and a need to run the house your way and to have everything done the way you want it to be. It is unlikely that you would be unfaithful, because it goes against the grain for you to behave in a sneaky behind-the-back manner. You are so loyal that you will stay in a situation and try to make it work, probably long after someone else would have walked out.

You may not rush into romance, so the chances are that you choose the right partner in the first place and enjoy a long and happy partnership. When you feel safe and secure, your sensuality will come to the fore, so you should have a happy sex life in a happy marriage-type relationship. Your lover will know where he or she stands, because you are honest and you prefer not to play games. However, you are prepared to fight for what you think is right, so any relationship with you will include a few arguments.

One of your greatest loves is nature. Water sign people are said to love the sea, but some love deserts. There is no rule about who loves what, but you certainly enjoy being outside and looking at a great view, and you enjoy visiting pretty gardens.

16

A Birth in the Hours Just Before Sunrise

This time takes us back to the first of the twelve houses and back to chapter 2. If you were born a little before dawn, place your Sun symbol a little below the dawn line. This puts your Sun in the first house. People do not always have an accurate time of birth, and some astronomical features can throw the timing off, so I suggest that you read the chapter that precedes this in addition to chapter 2.

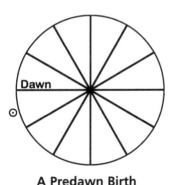

A Predawn Birth

17

A Quick Review

It is worth going over the salient points about the shape of the chart in relation to the time of birth again, so let us take another look at the Basic Time Chart and what it means in astrological terms.

An Astrology Chart

An astrologer's chart shows the twelve houses, which run in a counterclockwise direction from the ascendant.

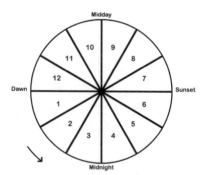

The Twelve Houses

The line that runs from the ascendant to the descendant divides the chart into two hemispheres. The line that runs from the midheaven to the nadir also divides the chart into two hemispheres.

If you were born with the Sun in the left hemisphere, you are self-reliant and your opinions and actions may change the lives of others. You were born between midnight and noon.

A Sun in the right hemisphere means that other people will have a powerful influence on you. The opinions, behavior, and actions of your lovers and partners (even working partners) will affect your moods and opinions. You were born between noon and midnight.

The upper hemisphere is concerned with public events and events outside the family circle, so if you have the Sun here, what you do in the world at large and what happens there may influence your life. You were born between sunrise and sunset.

The lower hemisphere relates to the home and the family, so if your Sun is here, the events that are close to home will always be important. Family members will influence you by their opinions, behavior, and activities. You were born between sunset and sunrise.

The Twelve Houses and the Four Angles

The Ascendant

The ascendant is the starting point on a chart; the sign it is in and any planets that are in its neighborhood will have a profound influence on you. This area of the chart refers to your childhood and the experiences that helped to shape you. The ascendant is also the cusp of the twelfth and first houses. If your Sun is here, you were born at or around sunrise.

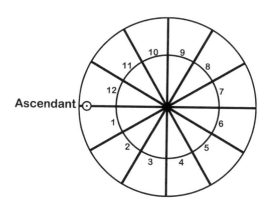

The First House

The first house rules a person, his or her health, appearance, body, his or her childhood influences, and his or her early programming. If your Sun is here, you were been born before sunrise.

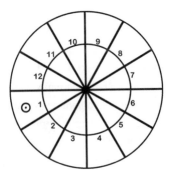

First House

The Second House

The second house rules what a person owns in terms of goods and money, but it also rules his or her value system and the things that he or she considers important. This also symbolizes the image that the person displays to others, or how others choose to see him or her. If your Sun is here, you were been born well before dawn, halfway between midnight and sunrise.

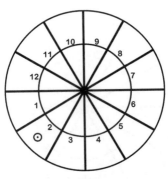

Second House

The Third House

The third house rules relationships with siblings and neighbors, communication, and mobility. It concerns the way a person gets around locally and local matters generally. It also rules basic education, literacy, numeracy, and dexterity. If your Sun is here, you were born during the night, in the very early hours of the morning.

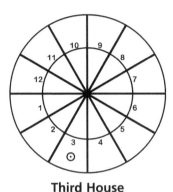

Third House

The Nadir or Immum Coeli (IC)

The nadir marks the bottom of the chart and is the cusp between the third and fourth houses. If your Sun is here, you were born at midnight.

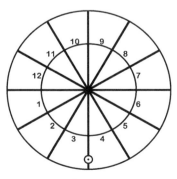

IC Placement

The Fourth House

The fourth house rules the past, the roots, or heritage, family background, and culture. It is concerned with family matters and parents—especially the mother or the one who nurtured the subject, whoever that happened to be. If your Sun is here, you were born before midnight.

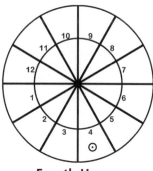

Fourth House

The Fifth House

The fifth house rules creativity in all its forms, so it can relate to creative enterprises, business, creating a beautiful home, and children. It also rules fun, leisure time, games and sports that are enjoyable, holidays, and love affairs. If your Sun is here, you were born halfway between sunset and midnight.

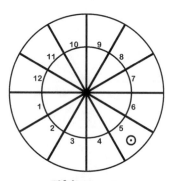

Fifth House

The Sixth House

The sixth house is concerned with work, employers and employees, and all matters relating to health. It can include an interest in small animals and such things as craft work or handiwork. If your Sun is here, you were born some time after sunset.

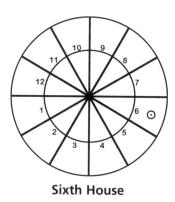

Sixth House

The Descendant

The descendant line is the cusp of the sixth and seventh houses. If your Sun is here, you were born at sunset.

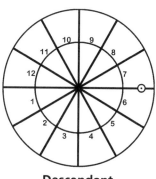

Descendant

The Seventh House

The seventh hosue rules open relationships such as love partnerships and business colleagues, but it also rules open enemies. It shows where a person tries to find a balance in his or her life. If your Sun is here, you were born before sunset.

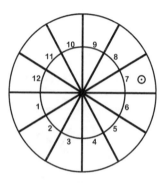

Seventh House

The Eighth House

The eighth house rules a number of important matters, especially shared resources and joint ownership. It relates to such things as mortgages, joint resources, taxes, inheritance, big business, and anything else that is not totally under a person's own control. It is concerned with relationships, birth, death, and sex. Things that are hidden and mysterious can be found here, whether this be hidden resentment at events of the past or an interest in spiritual and occult matters. If your Sun is here, you were born halfway between midday and sunset.

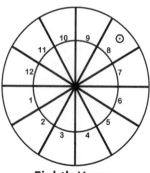

Eighth House

The Ninth House

The ninth rules expansion, so it encompasses mental expansion in the form of higher education and all forms of teaching and learning. The need for justice exerts itself here, so there is an attachment to the law. This house is also associated with spirituality and travel— in short, anything that expands one's experience of life. If your Sun is here, you were born shortly after midday.

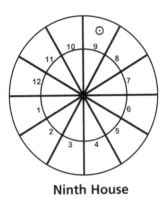

Ninth House

The Midheaven or Medium Coeli (MC)

This line marks the cusp of the ninth and tenth houses. If your Sun is here, you would have been born at midday.

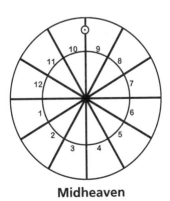

Midheaven

The Tenth House

The tenth house rules father figures, authority figures, power figures such as superiors at work, and those who have a high status in the subject's society. It also rules the career or any other kind of aspiration, status, and position in life. If your Sun is here, you were born shortly before midday.

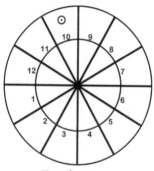

Tenth House

The Eleventh House

The eleventh rules acquaintances, those whom the subject meets socially, fellow members of clubs and societies and influential, high-status, or even political contacts that might be of help to the subject. It also rules any unconventionality, or even eccentricity and one's hopes and wishes. If your Sun is here, you were born halfway between sunrise and midday.

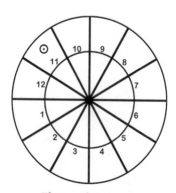

Eleventh House

The Twelfth House

On one hand the twelfth house can be a very strategic house that shows intuition and a capacity for forward thinking and political chess game playing, but it can also show a person's self-undoing if he or she carries things too far. There are secrets here; planets here show whether a person has an interest in mystical, psychic, or other alternative matters. If your Sun is here, you were born shortly after sunrise.

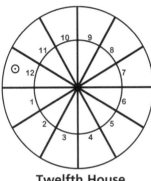

Twelfth House

The Ascendant—Again

This takes us back to the starting point once again. If you were born with your Sun here, you were born at sunrise.

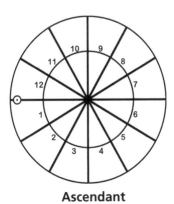

Ascendant

18

Your Sun Sign

This chapter gives you the opportunity to check out the Sun signs for your friends and loved ones. If you blend the Sun sign with the birth time characteristics, you will get a rounded picture of each person's basic nature. You will also find at-a-glance Sun and birth time combinations in chapter nineteen.

The calendar dates shown below for each sign are approximations, as the dates vary from year to year by a couple of days. If you are born within a few days of a sign change, check out both Sun signs to see which one is more like you; you may also find that some characteristics of both signs fit your nature.

Aries
Ruled by Mars
March 21 to April 20

Yours is a masculine fire sign and your symbol is the ram. This combination gives you courage, a love of adventure, energy, initiative, and a determination to live life to the fullest. You may look laid back and even docile at times, and you do not have a loud voice, but you are extremely competitive and this can take unwary folk by surprise. You play every game to win, and while this brings you considerable success, it can cost you the trust and affection of true friends.

You love your home. Whether it is a complete mess or a palace, it is yours and you will resist interference in your domestic life. The chances are that you are quite competent at do-it-yourself jobs, but you may go about them too quickly and without enough thought or preparation. You have a tendency to grab whatever tool or piece of equipment is handy to complete a job.

Despite being somewhat impulsive, you do not take chances where it matters. You can stay in a mundane job or even one where the people around you are unpleasant to you, if you need to the money badly enough. However, like most people, you prefer to be in a happy environment, and you are particularly suited to the position of supervisor. You need an outlet for your competitiveness, so a sporting hobby is a necessity. Many of you love to be a fan of sports and especially of car racing, even if you do not actually take part yourself.

You are extremely sociable, and under certain circumstances you can be the life and soul of the party. You do not sit around indoors much, and you need something to look forward to on weekends and evenings. When you get too old to run around on the sports field, you may sing in a choir or take up ballroom or old-time dancing. You are happy to spend money on holidays and entertainment, but you can be surprisingly stingy when it comes to boring necessities.

In love, you are ardent and keen, but you find it hard to be faithful, as you can fall in and out of love quite easily. You may need to experiment quite wildly where sex is concerned, and this will obviously lead to adventures and situations from which it is hard to extricate yourself. Well, at least you will know at the end of your life that you have lived!

Taurus
Ruled by Venus
April 21 to May 21

Yours is a feminine earth sign and your symbol is the bull. You are patient, thorough, and reliable. You do not change jobs or partners often, and you like your life to be much the same from one day to the next. However, you do enjoy travel and vacations that offer you a change of scene and a few unexpected events in a form that you can handle. Oddly enough, you can cope with surprising news better than most people can, and it takes a lot to upset your equilibrium. You hate to rush into major decision making, because you prefer to give important matters a lot of thought before taking action.

You are intensely loyal to your family and to your partner, so it is highly unlikely that you would stray or be unfaithful. The most important thing for you is to be happy and comfortable in your home, surrounded by your family, eating and entertaining friends as part of a loving and happy group.

You may not have been the brainiest student in school when you were young, but your teachers respected your common sense and reliability. The surprising thing is the way that you blossom later in life, and you can end up richer and with more success than many of your cleverer friends. Your mind is surprisingly shrewd and you understand far more than people outside your family realize. You think in a sensible and logical way, so you usually come to the right conclusion.

You have a terrific eye for what looks good, and whether you build a home, create a garden, or make a cake, it looks good and it fulfills its function perfectly. You have "safe" hands, and you rarely drop or break things, so you keep your goods and possessions in near perfect condition for many years. You are a careful driver.

In business, you can be surprisingly ambitious, but you are not prone to running after get-rich-quick schemes. You prefer to work at a steady job, which may be a blue-collar or hands-on kind of job. The world of banking and finance can attract you, though, so you might work in that field, slowly climbing the ladder of promotion. Your practical nature, combined with artistic talent, can lead to jobs that require a good eye, safe hands, and common sense.

Gemini
Ruled by Mercury
May 21 to June 21

Gemini is a masculine air sign, and your symbol is the twins. You can do six things at once while chatting on the phone at the same time! You need a great deal of variety in your life or you become bored and restless. You look for work that involves you in a variety of activities during the course of the day, and you prefer to work as part of a group than to be alone. You are happy in an office environment and you excel in accounting, record keeping, reception, and telephone work. Too much repetition in your daily life can make you turn right off.

Your quick wits mean that you can do things at a speed that others can only envy, and you are able to change direction just as quickly. If someone offers you the opportunity to drop the chores and go somewhere interesting, you will have your coat on and be ready to go at a moment's notice. Your logical mind does not inhibit your intuitive powers, though, so you can sum others up very quickly, and this can make you an excellent psychologist. However, while you can solve everybody else's problems you find it difficult to come to grips with your own. You can be a terrible worrier, sending yourself into neurotic anxiety over matters that are not worth worrying about. Here is one tip that I have often found useful when I have found myself worrying over nothing: if something is unlikely to matter in a year's time, it really does not matter at all.

You have a reputation for flirtatiousness but you are unlikely to follow up a good old flirting session with action, and what others take for sexual interest is often no more than fun and friendliness on your part. Communicating with others is a major part of your working day as well as your social life. If you can combine the two, you really have it made.

Cancer
Ruled by the Moon
June 22 to July 23

Cancer is a feminine water sign whose symbol is the crab. This makes you sensitive, sympathetic, and caring, but you reserve the bulk of your charitable instincts for members of your family. How you are with others depends on your mood, because you can be a sympathetic listener with a knack for comforting those who are unhappy. On the other hand, you can be incredibly hurtful and unpleasant. You may look soft, but your aggression and obstinacy can surprise others, especially those who try to attack any member of your family.

Many of you are shrewd and clever businesspeople, and you can make a success of a business where you deal with the public and supply people with their requirements. Many of you have small businesses of your own, especially shops or agencies. One typical Cancerian trait is the ability to cope with any amount of noise and chaos while at work, but you need a peaceful and organized home. Yours is a very domestic sign and you may be a very keen cook. You pay attention to proper nutrition, so you and your family eat well. I have noticed that most Cancerians drink little or no alcohol. It seems to upset your delicate stomach, so you are probably right to avoid it.

You prefer to keep both business and personal matters within the family as far as possible, and you do not like washing your dirty laundry in public. You may be thrifty in small ways, generous in big ones and you hate to waste money, but if times are hard, you can usually count on friends and relatives for support. They can also count on you for support when they need it.

You tend to look backward rather than forward, and while this can be healthy in some ways, for instance, by keeping photographs and mementos, it can be unhealthy if you find it hard to forget past hurts. History fascinates you, and you may collect antiques, coins, or other objects that have a story or a history attached to them. You do not throw much away; that is for sure.

Leo
Ruled by the Sun
July 23 to August 23

Leo is a masculine fire sign whose symbol is the lion. All Leos have high standards; you do not like to let yourselves or anyone else down. You try to do everything to the best of your ability and you may actually be too reliable and responsible for your own good. You can be a workaholic who maintains high standards both at work and in the home. You do not set out to impress others or to make them envy you, but if they become jealous or irritated by your capability or success, you cannot understand their reaction. After all, they could do what you do if they wanted to, couldn't they?

You can work as part of a team and even cope with menial jobs, but you are far more comfortable when in charge of a project. You cannot stand it when others treat you with contempt. You see through it when others pretend to be making a joke at your expense but really intend to ridicule you. You can become surprisingly downhearted, but you do not usually stay depressed for long and your confidence usually returns quickly. You can be very irritable when things go wrong and quite sarcastic when ill, under pressure, or overtired, but most of the time you are sunny and cheerful.

Generosity is your middle name and you are quick to help others, but you do have to learn not to give too much of your money and possessions away to others, because they soon learn to take advantage of you. You are an excellent host and an understanding listener to friends or relatives who may need help, so if someone is in trouble, you will do all you can to help.

You like the best of everything and you will not waste money on shoddy goods. You would rather go without something than buy poor-quality items. You are extremely friendly, sociable, and loyal to your friends. You will put up with a lot from others, but you will not put up with ridicule or betrayal or with those who criticize behind your back.

There is a childlike quality about you, and while you can be extremely businesslike outside the home, you love to curl up with your partner and make love. You enjoy having a good laugh with your partner. You love to play with your children, and you find it easy to enter their world and to spend a little time being young with them. You are fond of sports, and while you are quite competitive, you are not the type who has to win at all costs; you enjoy the game for its own sake, because having fun and participating in the game is more important to you than winning it. You also enjoy the friendship and social life that surround sporting hobbies.

Virgo
Ruled by Mercury
August 24 to September 23

Yours is a feminine earth sign and your symbol is the virgin. You are often defined as being cool, controlled, modest, and sexless, but how can this be so when yours is an earthy sign, associated with the ripeness of the harvest? You have very high standards of honesty and decency and a great deal of self-discipline, and you can keep your nose to the grindstone even if a job becomes boring. You are the artisan of the zodiac and you can cope with detailed work as long as it provides you with mental stimulation.

Some Virgos are very shy, and this can make you appear standoffish, but once people get to know you, they discover your wonderful sense of humor and your kind heart. Cruelty upsets you and you cannot watch the nastier items of news on the television. You prefer to be kind to others than to hurt them, and your own supersensitive nature makes you very nervous when around unkind or offensive people. However, if someone upsets you, your excellent grasp of language and your quick mind mean that you can be extremely hurtful in return.

Your partner will need to understand that you are not overly tactile, so holding hands on the sofa does not come easily to you. You prefer to show your love in practical ways, either by doing things for your loved one or by actual lovemaking. In deep relationships, you need the warmth and reassurance of a constant and steady partner. You are happier in the background than in the foreground of life, so, to some extent, you do not mind if your partner is more outgoing than you are, or even if he or she is a little bit bossy or apt to take charge of things.

Most Virgos are health-conscious and some of you are real hypochondriacs, while others are just a bit fussy about what they eat. Others seem to come from the opposite extreme, rarely mentioning their health and being happy to eat whatever is put in front of them. This is one of those polar situations, where people of the same Sun sign go from one extreme to the other. Sports are not at the top of your list of activities; you would rather read a good book.

Libra
Ruled by Venus
September 24 to October 24

Yours is a masculine air sign, symbolized by the scales. Your sign is contradictory, because the scales seem to suggest two different kinds of personality, both of which are typically Libran. Venus is a gentle, beauty-loving, self-indulgent planet, but your sign is also cardinal, suggesting that you like to think up new ideas and make them succeed. No wonder yours is such a confusing sign—and sometimes you are as confused as everyone else. No wonder you dislike making choices and decisions! You need time to think matters over and to weigh things up in your Libran scales. You hate it when others rush you, but once you have made a decision, only the equivalent of a nuclear bomb blast could persuade you to change your mind.

Some of you are gentle, peace-loving, and not very interested in a career, but others become heads of large enterprises. Some of you need little more than a happy partnership, a pleasant job, and enough money to live on. All Librans can be lazy at times. If you are the ambitious type, you can do very well in your chosen profession. You are all excellent conversationalists, and you are welcome at any social gathering due to your happy smile, your pleasant and friendly manner, and your niceness. At home, you can be extremely grumpy, especially if you mask your true feelings during your working day. Sometimes you can be downright unreasonable, and when you are in the mood, you can argue someone's ear off. Your talent for argument is useful in any negotiating situation, as you can often see ways of going about things that are good for all the parties involved. However, this trait can be a marriage breaker if you cannot stop doing it when you are at home.

Librans of both sexes are very domesticated, and you can happily cope with running a household, even down to handling quite extensive do-it-yourself jobs. Many of you are good cooks; indeed, one Libran friend of mine makes killer pancakes! You need pleasant surroundings and you may spend quite a bit of money on a stereo system. Whether married or living with someone on a permanent basis or as a part-time lover, you can be a wonderfully relaxed companion who makes the home a pleasant and comfortable place.

Scorpio
Ruled by Pluto and Mars
October 24 to November 22

Yours is a feminine water sign whose symbol is the scorpion. Astrology books give your sign a bad name, which, in my opinion, is undeserved. The reality is that you are a hardworking and honest member of the community, whose greatest interest is the happiness of your family. Loyalty is your middle name, and this is the case both within the family and at work. You work hard for your employers, and as long as they are reasonably decent toward you, you can stay happily in the same job for many years. Some of you reach the top of your profession, but many of you prefer to be in a partnership or to be slightly below the top level. In a way, you are happiest when you lead from behind and act as the power behind the throne. You can be a little manipulative, but your intentions are usually honorable.

Many of you like to have a dramatic lifestyle, and you love to talk to your relatives, friends, and colleagues about your latest drama. Scorpios are supposed to be secretive, but they are only secretive about certain things; most of the time they are too open, if anything.

If a member of your family is in trouble, you will be the first on the scene to try to put things right. Nobody is better than you are in a crisis. Perhaps this is what makes so many of you excellent emergency-room nurses and doctors. You are slow to trust others in anything other than a superficial matter, so there are always some aspects of your life that you do not allow others to know about. Some Scorpios prefer the company of animals to that of people, and even people-loving Scorpios love animals. None of you can bear to see an animal suffer.

Sagittarius
Ruled by Jupiter
November 23 to December 21

Yours is a masculine fire sign, ruled by the archer or the centaur. You need personal freedom, and you cannot stand anyone who gives you the third degree about where you are going and how long you are likely to be. You cannot cope with people who want to run your life. You may choose to live a perfectly conventional life with a home, family, and pets, or you may prefer to have friends and lovers, but to live alone. Some Sagittarians can be great as friends, but too awkward, selfish, or downright peculiar to live in a normal family situation, so they are better off alone. Many start out by marrying and having children but lose contact with all these people later in life.

Many of you have jobs that take you from place to place, visiting different areas during your working week. You enjoy the traveling and the variety of new faces that you encounter during your working day. If you work in one place, the job must have plenty of variety and an opportunity to talk to many people during the day. You are a great traveler, and if you cannot travel for your work, you save your money for at least one interesting journey each year. Friends and family members are very important to you, and you love to visit your loved ones or to have them stay with you. This adds variety to your life in a particularly pleasant way.

You enjoy keeping yourself up-to-date with the latest trends. Your outlook is forward-looking and modern, and you do not dwell on the past too much if you can help it. Your fine mind ensures that you keep learning and taking an interest in all that is going on around you. Many of you have a deep interest in philosophy or religion, but it is unlikely to be the same religion that your family embraced. Astrology and spiritual thought interest many of you, and the chances are that you have a good deal of knowledge about these subjects. Many Sagittarians are excellent clairvoyants or mediums. Many of you are excellent at sports and games, and you find an hour or two at the local gym a good outlet for your considerable energies.

Yours is a happy-go-lucky outlook and you worry less about money and the future than most other people do. You know you will always land on your feet.

Capricorn
Ruled by Saturn
December 22 to January 20

Yours is a feminine earth sign whose symbol is the goat. You are ambitious and hardworking, and some of you can be a little too serious for your own good. Nevertheless, many of you have the ability to let your hair down and party the night away to your heart's content. You do not enjoy it when others rush you into things, and you like to do your work and your chores at your own pace. Some Capricorns are painfully shy and retiring, while others are surprisingly outgoing, but even the shy ones become more confident and outgoing in middle age. You are clever, but you use your intelligence in a practical way. Your brightness, coupled with your capacity for hard work and concentration, can bring you success in any number of fields. You can be quite tough in business, but your quiet and polite manner and gentle sense of humor help you to get your own way without upsetting others.

You can be a little too ambitious or too focussed on money, and this can alienate others, or leave your family wondering when you are likely to find enough time for them as well as for your work. If you are this type of Capricorn, you need to work on creating a certain balance in your life that allows for fun and relaxation as well as work, but this may be difficult for you, as you enjoy being productive and you like to end each day feeling that you have done something useful with it. Once you feel secure enough financially, your thoughts turn to the idea of traveling and of taking your family away for a nice vacation or two. You do not enjoy traveling alone; you prefer to take your partner and even a quite extended family along with you.

You take a responsible attitude to your personal relationships and to family life, and you would even do a good job of looking after stepchildren or in-laws if necessary. Many of you are extremely good-looking, and your slim figure and fine bone structure ensure that you stay that way far into your old age. You can be a bit of a flirt, but if you are in an important relationship, such flirting is innocent; you are intensely loyal to the one you love.

Aquarius
Ruled by Uranus and Saturn
January 21 to February 19

Yours is a masculine air sign whose symbol is the water carrier. Aquarians are different from just about everyone else, including all the other Aquarians, and this makes you hard to categorize. You are extremely independent and your mode of thinking is very individual. You value education highly—both as the road to success, wealth, and independence, and for its own sake. You are interested in everything and you love to have friends around you who converse with you about a whole variety of subjects. If you have a family, you will ensure that they get all the education that they can bear and even your long-suffering partner is encouraged to read thought-provoking books or to take courses to keep up with your restless mind.

Aquarians work in any number of careers, but anything that allows you to communicate with others is bound to be a favorite. You may work in the public sector and in technical jobs of one kind or another, with computers being a favorite choice. You may choose to teach or write for a living, and many of you drift into self-employment. You have the most original mind of the zodiac and you may spend your life solving problems or inventing new and original systems. Despite the reputation that your sign has for being intellectual and mentally active, you also have a strong physical side to you that expresses itself in such tasks as do-it-yourself or even quite large building projects. Many of you work as self-employed engineers or building craftspeople.

You have a broad mind and an easygoing attitude regarding other people's eccentricities. You do not necessarily see your own behavior as eccentric, but you are the first to say that you are different from the herd. The sign of Aquarius is particularly associated with astrology; indeed there are many Aquarian astrologers. Other typical interests can include environmental issues, Egyptology, magic, the Tarot, and alternative health and healing.

You look into everything and you take every idea seriously, but you form your own opinions and stick with them thereafter. Like the other two air signs, you can argue someone's ear off, but you rarely do this to hurt others, only to have fun in debate or when you need to protect yourself.

Pisces
Ruled by Jupiter and Neptune
February 20 to March 20

This is a feminine water sign whose symbol is two fish, tied together and swimming in opposite directions. Yours is a strange nature, as it carries within it so many contradictions. You may be efficient and capable in some ways, but chaotic and muddled in others, and you can switch between these patterns in the blink of an eye. The fact of the matter is that you are extremely sensitive and highly intuitive and there are times when this psychic ability takes over from your more logical side. You may embark on a course of action, only to change your mind halfway through because it simply does not feel right.

Your nature is strongly sympathetic toward others, and you rush to help or heal those who are in difficulty, sometimes at the expense of your own family's needs or your own need for peace or rest. Many of you work in the caring profession, as teachers or nurses, or in animal welfare, and these careers offer you the opportunity to express your compassion. Some of you become martyrs to your family, or fall under the thumb of a stronger personality. However, you can survive even the most difficult of circumstances.

Many of you express your wonderful artistic streak in the work you choose to do, and, if so, the chances are that you do not earn very much for your efforts. To some extent, your values are more spiritual than material and the need to satisfy your creative urge is more important to you than earning a high income.

There is a strong mystical side to you, drawing you to religious, spiritual, or new age ideas, and many of you work as spiritual healers, mediums, and Tarot readers. You are drawn to natural or alternative health therapies and you may eventually spend time working in such fields. One natural outlet for your talents is reflexology, because this involves treating the feet, and your ruling planet, Neptune, rules the feet. Many Pisceans work as exorcists of one kind or another, either helping lonely spirits on their way or removing them from the lives and bodies of those whom they have invaded.

19

Sun Signs and Birth Times at a Glance

Here are quick clues to each Sun sign character, allied to the eight divisions of the Basic Time Chart. I have repeated the illustration here for you. Remember to deduct one hour for daylight saving or British summer time births.

The Basic Time Chart

The Basic Time Chart is like a twenty-four clock, but it shows dawn on the left-hand side, midday at the top, dusk on the right, and midnight at the bottom. The area above the horizontal line represents daytime and the part below it represents nighttime. Make a photocopy of the chart and draw your Sun sign on it along with the notes as you read.

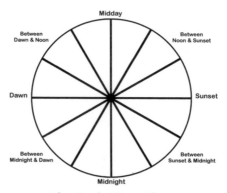

The Basic Time Chart

A Sunrise Birth

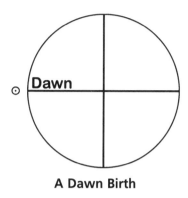

A Dawn Birth

Aries

Courage and adventurousness, impetuosity, and haste characterize your nature, so you rush in where angels fear to tread.

Taurus

This powerful combination makes you unstoppable, and probably highly successful at anything to which you put your mind. Try to consider the needs of less powerful loved ones and colleagues.

Gemini

You think and act at the speed of light and your intellect will take you far, but you must try to think before you speak—or act.

Cancer

You push hard for what you need and also for what your family needs. You can use information that comes your way to your advantage, but you must guard against spreading gossip.

Leo

There is nothing you can't achieve once you set your mind to it, but success can go to your head and make you overbearing and arrogant.

Virgo

Your clever brain will get you anywhere that you want to be, but you may become convinced that your way is the only way to do things.

Libra

This placement makes you unusually decisive and firm, but you can also become a bully if you are not careful. Remember to consider the feelings of others.

Scorpio

Your determination to get things done and to finish what you start is admirable, but your loud voice and displays of temper can frighten others—especially children.

Sagittarius

You feel so deeply about some issues that you can make them your life's work, but you must guard against becoming a soapbox bore.

Capricorn

Your drive for power and position will take you far, and your idealism is to be applauded, but you can become so wrapped up in what you do that you forget to have fun.

Aquarius

If anybody can save the planet, you can, but you may become so single-minded that you forget to give time to your friends and loved ones.

Pisces

Your search for the meaning of life and answers to life's mysteries will give you an interesting life, but you may become so eccentric that you will find it hard to fit in.

A Birth Between Sunrise and Noon

A Midmorning Birth

Aries

Your idealism could make you a catalyst for major change for the better. Your political arena is likely to be in your neighborhood.

Taurus

This placement adds an interest in books, music, and ideas to practicality and common sense, so you should be able to make a success of any creative venture.

Gemini

Your mind goes at full speed and you can talk someone's ear off while doing six other things at the same time.

Cancer

This placement makes you less inclined to hole up at home and focus solely on your family, so it adds friendliness and breadth of mind.

Leo

Inventiveness, originality, and the ability to finish what you start combine to make you a success at anything that you set your mind to.

Virgo

This combination adds to your considerable intelligence and it also makes you humanitarian and caring, so you can become a force for good in the world.

Libra

You will become an advocate for those who need a voice. This could take you into legal or advisory work.

Scorpio

This is a pleasant combination, as it gives you intense loyalty to your friends and a desire to make the world a better place.

Sagittarius

Your idealism is admirable, but it can be a little over the top, so try to combine a little common sense and a more laid-back attitude to life.

Capricorn

You are unlikely to be one of the strong, silent types of Capricorn, as you love to chat and giggle with your friends. When working, you focus on what needs to be done.

Aquarius

You have an original and inventive brain, but you may lack grounding or common sense, so try to see things from a more basic point of view from time to time.

Pisces

You may be too dreamy and idealistic for your own good. Try to maintain a grip on reality.

A Midday Birth

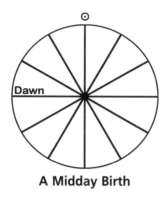

A Midday Birth

Aries

Reach for the skies because there is nothing you cannot achieve if you set your mind to it. However, if you do something dishonest or dishonorable, it will come out in public.

Taurus

You may not look like a candidate for the top job, but fate can take you there. Once you reach the top, you will do your best to stay there.

Gemini

Your wit and sparkle will make you a social success, while your intellect could take you to the top in an area of communication.

Cancer

Your patriotism and attention to duty could make you a military leader—or just a great family person.

Leo

Your charisma and love of life can take you to the top in the entertainment industry or some aspect of the arts. You succeed at anything that you put your mind to.

Virgo

Your nature impels you to spend your life in the service of others, and your powerful personality can be a force for good in the world.

Libra

If you are drawn to the world of music and entertainment, you could reach the top. If your aim is business success or a happy family life, you should achieve this too.

Scorpio

You could become a top surgeon or an inventive engineer, but whatever you choose to do, you will do it well.

Sagittarius

Your desire is to open the eyes of others to all the wonderful possibilities that life holds, so you will be a great teacher and an inspiration to others.

Capricorn

Whether you choose the world of politics, business, or finance, you have the capacity to reach the top, but you must try to relax and have fun as well.

Aquarius

You may join a group or organization and then become its leader and its inspiration, but you will also seek to enjoy life and have many friendships.

Pisces

A combination of intuition and business sense can take you a long way, but you mustn't allow your family to drain your finances or your energy. I have known quite a few successful professional psychics with this sign-time combination.

A Birth Between Midday and Sunset

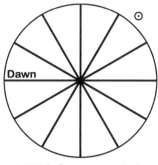

A Midafternoon Birth

Aries

This placement could make you a military leader, a surgeon, or an investigator, an espionage agent, or even a sex god or goddess. Whatever you choose to do, your life will never be boring.

Taurus

You have an instinct for finance, so you could work in the area of home loans or the stock market. Even if you choose a different type of career, you will have a good grip of practical matters.

Gemini

Past hurts and resentment can make you miserable at times, so try to put the past behind you and do what you can to make yourself and others happy.

Cancer

Your emotions are so powerful that you sometimes act on instinct and forget to stop and think. Always sleep on major decisions to give yourself time to cool off before taking action.

Leo

This placement gives you glamour and charisma, talent, and luck, so you could reach a position of power or become a star in the acting profession.

Virgo

Your good looks and smoldering sexuality may lead to an acting career, while your brain might make you a wonderful doctor.

Libra

Your powerful sex drive will lead to many interesting adventures, and you may break a few hearts before you finally settle down.

Scorpio

Your powerful personality can make you an amazing force for good, but you could just as easily turn to criminality and the dark side of life. Stay in the light.

Sagittarius

This placement adds a welcome dose of determination and capability to your clever brain, so it can lead to success.

Capricorn

Your sure touch with practical matters allies itself to intuition and the ability to see through others, so this should help you to attain your desires.

Aquarius

You might become an archeologist, a historian, an Egyptologist, or even a space traveler. Your life will never be ordinary.

Pisces

This is an excellent placement for a psychic medium or remote-viewing specialist. You artistic talents will also take you far.

A Sunset Birth

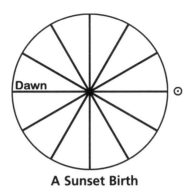

A Sunset Birth

Aries

You work hard on behalf of others, and while you achieve what you set out to do, you might end up resenting the fact that you have neglected your own needs.

Taurus

Despite your desire for a happy marriage, this may elude you the first time around. You will enjoy working as a part of a team.

Gemini

You may try to live through a partner or expect others to make you happy, so you should endeavor to become more self-reliant and independent.

Cancer

Your business instincts allied to your ways with people can take you far in some line of work that involves dealing with the public.

Leo

Your powerful personality and desire for success will take you to the top, but you must guard against walking all over weaker or less effective people.

Virgo

Yours is an intellectual sign, but this birth time adds artistic ability, so you can combine both of these talents for success.

Libra

Singing, music, and art are close to your heart, so you might pursue a career in an artistic field, or at least enjoy these things as a pastime.

Scorpio

Romance and love are terribly important for you, so you will definitely have a number of grand passions during the course of your life.

Sagittarius

You are such a happy, friendly person that you will hardly ever need to sit around at home or be lonely.

Capricorn

This placement adds an appreciation of art and beauty, so you could make a career out of creating or marketing art, music, or entertainment.

Aquarius

Your natural inventiveness allies to artistic appreciation, and this could make you an excellent fashion designer or sculptor.

Pisces

You live for love and romance, and if you meet the right kind of partner, you will have an exceedingly happy life.

A Birth Between Sunset and Midnight

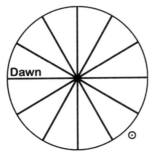

A Midevening Birth

Aries
If you have career ambitions, you will be drawn to teaching or possibly to some branch of the entertainment industry, but you could actually be more into family life than a career.

Taurus
Although you probably work outside the home, you are less interested in a career than in making a happy home and looking after children.

Gemini
There is a pleasantly childlike quality in you, making you a happier personality than most Geminis are, and you might even work with small children or young people.

Cancer
The two things that are closest to your heart are your children and any creative enterprises that you pursue.

Leo
You have a loving heart and you will do your very best for your partner, children, family, and friends. Your charisma could lead you into the entertainment industry as a career or as a pastime.

Virgo

Your attention to detail, coupled with artistic and creative talent, could take you into writing and illustrating as a career. You have more fun than most Virgos do.

Libra

Being highly creative and also fond of a good time, you should have a happy life. You may prefer dating and socializing to marriage and a settled life.

Scorpio

Once you overcome an early lack of confidence, you will probably go into business and do very well. Your children will always be close to your heart.

Sagittarius

What a sunny personality you have! Much of your life will be spent making others happy, but you should also be happy and lucky yourself much of the time, as long as you don't allow yourself to get involved in gambling.

Capricorn

You are far more cheerful and outgoing than most Capricorns, and you could enjoy active sports and pastimes such as singing and dancing. You may work in the creative side of publishing.

Aquarius

Creative, original, inventive, and full of fun, you could do a great deal for children and young people. You may design computer games, toys, or children's games.

Pisces

Your artistic and creative nature could lead you into a career or a pastime in the world of entertainment. You love children and will enjoy looking after your own and your grandchildren.

A Midnight Birth

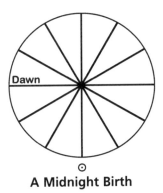

A Midnight Birth

Aries

Unusually for your sign, you opt for a quiet life, putting your family first and doing an ordinary job in an office, school, or cafeteria close to your home.

Taurus

Your social and working lives center on your home and family. You may enjoy running a small farm, flower shop, or animal shelter.

Gemini

If your family is all right and your job not overly demanding, you are happy. You need regular hours, plenty of sleep, and a quiet life.

Cancer

You can succeed in anything relating to property, from building to interior designing. You may read Tarot as a part-time occupation. Your family will always come before your job, though.

Leo

Your intuition and psychic interests will take you into the world of psychism, astrology, and related subjects, and you may make a living writing about such things.

Virgo

You can ally your intelligence, receptive mind, artistic inclinations, and interest in astrology to make a career in this field.

Libra

Your powerful instincts can take you far in business or industry, and you don't hesitate to use your psychic abilities to figure out who your friends and enemies are.

Scorpio

Your powerful psychism can make you see ghosts, but your equally powerful imagination can allow psychic phenomena to frighten you. Try to keep your feet on the ground. You will work in a caring or helping profession.

Sagittarius

You are bound to be interested in spiritual matters, and you could make an excellent spiritual teacher or healer. Your other work will involve travel and meeting many different people.

Capricorn

You can work happily in any large, global organization. Your spiritual interests could lead you to read, write, or produce books on esoteric subjects.

Aquarius

Before it became mundane and ordinary, you would have worked in the field of computing. Now you could work for any large organization, but you will always have interesting pastimes and outside interests.

Pisces

You could work in the medical or caring fields, but you are likely to be involved in psychism, spirituality, and spiritual healing.

A Birth Between Midnight and Sunrise

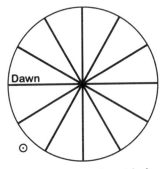

An Early Morning Birth

Aries

You would do well in a job that is a combination of working with numbers, helping others, and being part of a large organization—a hospital, perhaps. Your intuition is so powerful that you might work as a psychic in your spare time.

Taurus

An interest in domestic and household matters or market gardening could turn itself into a moneymaking career for you, as your natural shrewdness helps you to turn your ideas into gold.

Gemini

Your forte is people, so this talent could take you into psychiatry or journalism. You will always have lots of friends, and you will not spend much time sitting around at home.

Cancer

Your impulsiveness might land you in trouble at times, so try to think before you take on a new project or a new person, because a little forethought could save you from getting into hot water later.

Leo
You have an eye for new ideas and new technology. They say that "it's not rocket science," but in your case, it could well be!

Virgo
An analytical mind and an interest in technology could lead you into computer programming, systems analysis, or journalism.

Libra
If you are career-minded, you will want to work in a field that provides important things for the population at large. I knew one Libra with this birth time who worked in the field of nuclear energy.

Scorpio
Your interest in people, combined with a talent for medicine, could take you into surgery, psychiatry, or complementary medicine.

Sagittarius
Extreme individuality can take you into unusual, interesting kinds of work. A happy personal life and many good friends are likely.

Capricorn
Your public relations skills, common sense, and idealism would make you a wonderful fund-raiser for a charity, but you may need a mundane job as well. You take good care of your family.

Aquarius
Truly individual, you could fall into any unusual line of work or into local politics. You may not bother with a conventional family life, but live in a commune of some kind instead.

Pisces
The worlds of mysticism and complementary medicine interest you—perhaps as your main job, or in your spare time while enjoying a job in sales or public relations.

20

The Ascendant or Rising Sign

The words *ascendant* and *rising sign* mean the same thing. Astrologers often talk about Taurus rising, Libra rising, and so on.

Those of you who know little or nothing about astrology will be amazed when you discover the influence that the ascendant exerts on your character. It is often (but not always) more obvious on first acquaintance than the Sun sign. When someone at a party asks what sign you are, they are asking about your Sun sign, but if you were to ask them what sign they thought you were, they would probably pick up your ascendant.

The Sun sign depends on your date of your birth, but the ascendant depends on your date, place, and time of birth. I provide a rough table for finding the ascendant in this book, but you can use a free astrology service—details are usually available on www.sashafenton.com—for exact data.

The ascendant and the first astrological house reflect the programming that you received in childhood, showing the way your parents, relatives, siblings, teachers, and friends behaved toward you and what they required from you. It can show how you acted and reacted toward them. This programming often remains with you for the rest of your life. So think back for a moment and see whether you can remember what you once thought you might grow up and become—and whether you did what you thought you would do.

I could say a great deal about the astronomy and astrology of the ascendant, but technical details are beyond the scope of a book of this kind. However, here are a few simple points for you to keep in mind:

(1) The rising sign is important in its own right, but it also sets the starting position of the twelve astrological houses.

(2) The Sun and ascendant can only be in the same sign if you were born at dawn. Thus, if you were both Sun in Aries and Aries rising, you would be "double Aries."

(3) Some years ago, the late Charles Harvey ran a survey to discover whether people looked like their Sun sign, their ascendant, or something else. He discovered that around 45 percent of people look like their Sun sign, and another 45 percent look like their ascendant. Other factors influenced the remaining 10 percent.

So, now let us look at the way that your ascendant influences you. Bear in mind that if you were born toward the end of a rising sign, the next sign will occupy most of your first house, so you will need to read both signs. You will also find more about this subject in another of my books, *The Hidden Zodiac*.

Aries Rising

One or both parents may be domineering or unreasonable, and confrontations are particularly likely to occur when the child reaches his or her teens; he or she may then escape by leaving home when young, in order to get away from this parental pressure. Some Aries rising subjects will go into the armed forces to get away, while others marry and start a family while very young. Others will simply take off and establish a separate life from that of their parents. Choosing to leave or to stay and fight depends on the person's basic nature and on many factors in his or her horoscope. Often this subject is the oldest child in the family or one who does not quite fit in at home, or the one who somehow seems to set off peevish or domineering behavior in the parents. This person may be naturally rather self-centered, or he or she may develop a level of selfishness out of sheer self-preservation. The Aries rising person is usually of medium height, with a pale skin and ordinary looks.

Taurus Rising

In theory, this should be a pleasant sign to have around, but so often, something is askew in the subject's childhood. The childhood experiences make financial security or financial independence an imperative. Sometimes the child learns from his or her parents that a large and well-appointed house, lots of possessions and status symbols, along with plenty of money in the bank are the key to a happy life. This means that he or she chases after these things throughout adulthood, either by working for them or perhaps through marriage. However, Taurus around the ascendant adds a practical streak, along with creative talent and sociability, which, allied to a good head for money matters, endows this person with a great opportunity for worldly success. This is fine, but some who have this rising sign do not make it, and that makes them bitter. For some inexplicable reason, some people with this sign rising are selfish, argumentative, and unpleasant to be around. The Taurus rising subject usually may be quite slim, with a slight look of a bulldog about the mouth.

Gemini Rising

I call this the sign of the orphan, because even if the child is not actually abandoned, he or she probably feels this way. This rising sign denotes loneliness and difficulty in childhood. Even if there are people around, the child feels lonely and misunderstood. Even if the home life was good, this person would have felt alienated at school or elsewhere. Gemini rising children are friendly relaters and they lack the kind of caution that distances them from hurtful people or situations.

This child is talkative, and while our adult world welcomes communicators, schoolteachers frequently try to shut them up.

However, the parents do all they can to stimulate the child's intellect. Adults with Gemini rising can be cutting and far too quick to express an opinion, but usually only when they are being badly treated. Later in life, some of these subjects choose to marry partners who appear strong and confident, because they think that they will look after them. In some cases this works; in others it does not. Unless they can find the right outlet for their intelligence and talents, they continue to feel like a square peg in a round hole at work as well as at home. The Gemini rising child may be an only child, an unwanted child, or a late addition to parents who thought that they had completed their family and who are bored with the thought of bringing up yet another child. They may start out as parents who want a child, only to find the child an encumbrance or embarrassment later. The Gemini rising person is very thin when young and slim during midlife, but he or she can become quite plump later on, and sometimes has rather fine hair.

Cancer Rising

This can be an excellent rising sign or a surprisingly difficult one. The mother is a strong influence and often a strong role model. In some cases, the child's mother cares, but in others, she is a powerful and frightening figure. The Cancer rising child is often the older one, who takes the responsibility for looking after the younger members of the family. This person may go on later to marry a younger partner or one who is sick, insecure, or who needs mothering or supporting in other ways. The Cancer rising nature is cautious and sometimes quite suspicious of others. These people are deeply intuitive, and they only deal with those whom they can trust. Most have good business heads on their shoulders. They are capable and responsible with money and with other aspects of their lives. One fault that seems to beset some of these people is that of stinginess or a talent for spending large sums on one thing and being far too thrifty on others. As children, they sit at the back of the classroom and try to keep out of everyone's way. Some endure school and get out as soon as they can; others do quite well at school. The Cancer rising person is usually nice-looking, with a rounded face and figure. They often have plenty of slightly wavy hair.

Leo Rising

Children of this ascendant were wanted by their parents, but they may turn out to be such a handful that their parents tune them out or become tired of their company. In many cases, these children are extremely talented and good-looking, and their parents may push them to achieve great success, often in some artistic or show business field. There is no rule as to the child's position in a family, but he or she will certainly stand out in some way. He may be the only boy in a family of girls or vice versa, or the only one with artistic, musical, or creative talent in a rather ordinary family. The adult with this rising sign may suffer from the feeling that he or she did not quite make it; that, somehow, he or she did not reach the standard expected. These people can be self-centered. They can go through life as though they are acting a part rather than living in the real world. They can be defensive and hurtful when there is nothing to defend. As schoolchildren, these subjects can do very well or very badly, but they usually have some kind of talent that distinguishes them as being special. Leo rising people are good-looking and sometimes rather vain.

Virgo Rising

This difficult sign suggests that there was something wrong during childhood. The child may have been unwanted, but even when he or she is wanted, somehow, fate soon decrees that he or she gets in somebody's way. Sometimes the mother simply cannot cope, or is sickly or neurotic. The parents (especially the mother) are in some way detached or distanced from the child. This may be due to circumstances or due to the fact that the parents find something more interesting to do than bringing up a child. These children can be fussy and neurotic, especially over matters related to health or food, and they can become hypochondriacs. The child is clever, but he or she may be shy or backward in some way. Sometimes this child simply does not gel with the rest of the family. In other cases, his or her loud voice and fondness for speaking out irritates schoolteachers who spend years trying to shut him or her up. Virgo rising people do better in later life when their ability to sort, analyze, and investigate matters, and their habit of reading and studying deeply, stand them in good stead. These subjects can be confrontational, argumentative, and cutting when they feel the need to defend themselves. They often have pale skin, good bone structure, and dark hair, and they keep their good looks throughout life, as long as they do not gain too much weight.

Libra Rising

In theory, this is a pleasant sign to have, as the person is usually nice-looking and easygoing. The reality is that the father may have been absent during childhood for much or all of the time, and the child does not receive the love and guidance that he or she needs. If the mother is angry with the father during childhood, the child absorbs that anger as well. The child may be left to his or her own devices for much of the time or may be spoiled with material things, toys, and other goodies while missing true nurturing. A tendency to be lazy and to live in a dreamworld may make him or her something of a failure at school, and parents and teachers will not hesitate to point this out. In many cases, this type drifts easily through life. Some Libra rising subjects become bitter about the fact that society will not recognize their talents. These people are often charming, nice looking, charismatic, and attractive.

Scorpio Rising

The parents (especially the mother) are usually good, and they love the child, but there are often outside circumstances that make life difficult for these children or for their families. The problem may be poverty, sickness, or something else that makes them feel out of step with their peers. This breeds a cautious attitude, secrecy, and deep feelings that are kept hidden. These subjects develop a good deal of intuition, and they learn early to watch others and to keep their mouths shut. It takes a lot for these people to trust others and to open up to them about their true thoughts and feelings. They feel that there is more to everything than meets the eye. This may account for the large numbers of them who find their way into astrology and psychic work. Many of these subjects are only children, a different gender from their siblings, or in some other way a little different from others. Scorpio rising people can descend into dreadful moods, either becoming self-pitying or giving their partners the silent treatment. Scorpio rising people may be good-looking or really quite ordinary, but they have strong features and a direct gaze that is often described as "magnetic."

Sagittarius Rising

Many astrologers and people who are interested in spiritual matters have this sign rising or in some important place on their charts. The childhood seems to be reasonably happy, but the child is keen to leave home early and to experiment with different ideas from those that his parents and schoolteachers tried to force upon him or her. If the child grows up in a strongly religious atmosphere, he or she will almost inevitably reject these beliefs and look for meaning in other philosophies. This rising sign often belongs to a quite favored younger child in the family, who gets away with murder. Alternatively, this is the kind of child who makes friends with some other family and almost moves in with them, or in some other way finds reasons to spend as little time at home as possible. These people are kind, humorous, and sympathetic, but they can be tactless and extremely sarcastic, competitive, and hurtful when they feel the need. They are fairly tall and often quite plain, with a long jaw or a horsy face. Their friendly, humorous, and intelligent nature makes them popular.

Capricorn Rising

Capricorn rising signifies a hard childhood, but this is not necessarily due to bad parents or bad parenting. Sometimes there are many brothers and sisters in the family, but in other cases, poverty is a factor. The child learns early that money in the bank, a fully paid house, security, and a decent career are important. He or she may be hardworking and serious at a time when other youngsters are having fun. He or she takes life seriously and may feel a lack of something that other children have. In some cases, the Capricorn rising child is sickly; in others, he or she misses out on schooling. One redeeming feature for these children is that they often form excellent relationships with their grandparents and they therefore become more comfortable in the presence of older people than they do in the presence of those of their own age. Their lack of confidence and sometimes painful shyness means that they find personal relationships difficult, although if they find the right partner later in life, they make excellent relationships with all members of their families. These people can be cliquey, selfish, and unable to acknowledge the needs and feelings of others. They can look old when they are young and young when they are old, and their looks improve with age.

Aquarius Rising

Aquarius rising people may have an unusual character or an unusual way of looking at life. They learn to be independent early on, either because they have to stand on their own two feet or because their parents encourage them to do so. The childhood is usually pretty good, although there may be a level of instability that means that the child attends several different schools or lives in a variety of different places. The parents do all they can to ensure that the child receives a good education and plenty of mental stimulation. These subjects cannot swallow the opinions of others wholesale because they need to think things through and make up their own minds. They have a pleasant manner that endears them to others, and they have no trouble making new friends. They usually get along well in family life, as long as they do not end up with a partner who seeks to control them. Aquarius rising subjects keep their thoughts and feelings to themselves, but they often feel contempt for those around them. If necessary, they will cut themselves off completely from those who have hurt them. At school, they are not particularly successful in academic subjects, but they do well with technical topics. Some take to computing; others to auto mechanics or engineering. Still others are successful at sports. These people are taller than average and rather nice-looking, and they remain pretty attractive throughout life.

Pisces Rising

There is often an element of loneliness in this person's childhood, even if there are many brothers and sisters in the family. Sometimes this is due to a period of time in the hospital; sometimes it is the result of circumstances beyond anyone's control. The parents do their best, but they are often ineffective, so the child learns to cope alone. Despite the fact that the sign of Pisces is not associated with career or business success, this person often does rather well in life. The problem is that he or she may waste the gains that he or she makes by supporting a needy partner later in life. Pisces rising subjects usually have a prickly and hostile manner that makes them uncomfortable to be with. Perhaps this is some kind of defense mechanism, or maybe an inferiority complex. These people are at their happiest when they develop their artistic, musical, creative, or psychic talents, and once they achieve some success and their self-confidence develops, they become nicer to be with. These people tend to be pale-skinned and fair-haired. They look pleasantly ordinary.

21

Rectifying a Time of Birth

It is possible to rectify a time of birth to find the exact ascendant, but it is not an easy thing to do. There is some software available nowadays that helps with this, but only as part of a larger program, and it is not completely accurate. Unfortunately, it is hard to explain the technique to a non-astrologer, so I will not try to dumb this down. I suggest that you take this chapter to a skilled astrologer.

The starting point is to find the actual sign on the ascendant, and you do this by looking at a range of childhood situations and gradually eliminating those that do not fit. The section on the ascendant in this book will help, but it is worth buying several books on the rising sign so that you get a good grip on how each one manifests itself. Many people look or behave more like their ascendant than their Sun sign, so that can be helpful in some cases. Some people follow careers that link with their ascendant. I will give a very brief list of suggestions at the end of this chapter.

When you are satisfied that you have the right rising sign, you should set up a chart that places the ascendant halfway through that sign (at about 15 degrees). Then you should look at the MC (the medium coeli, or midheaven) and gradually progress it backward one degree at a time. One degree of arc represents one year of life. When the MC reaches a point where it makes a hard aspect to a planet or some other important feature on the chart, ask yourself whether something relevant happened during your childhood and at what date. If nothing comes to mind, then progress the MC forward and try again. A hard aspect to Mars suggests an accident or operation, and if you look at the sign that Mars is in, you might be able to determine which part of the body was affected. Aspects to the Moon might relate to your parents, moving to a new house, or a family upheaval, while aspects to Uranus or Pluto are always memorable. You will have to look at other transits in addition to the MC. This will locate the age of the person at the time of the event, which will then enable you to find the correct MC. Once you have done that, you can set the ascendant in its rightful position. If you are a few degrees off, keep looking at the events of your life as they unfold and watch the transits, progressions, and solar returns go by. This will help you to fix the ascendant accurately.

In some cases, a planet close to the ascendant will give a clue. When I rectified my ascendant, I discovered that Saturn was almost exactly on it, and that Pluto was my rising planet. My mother had an extremely hard labor; we both almost died. The Second World War was raging and bombs were falling; rationing was in full swing; and my father was away building Hurricane aircraft. My mother was lonely and up against a wall. Saturn in hard aspect to the ascendant fits this scenario—even more so in my case, as the cusp of my eighth house is ruled by Capricorn. Pluto links with the fact that people were dying all around us, and that my early life was marked by funerals as one member of our family after another died—including my father and uncle, both of whom were still very young.

Quick Clues

As promised, a table of quick clues to the ascendant is on the next page.

	CLUES TO THE ASCENDANT
SIGNS	**FACTORS**
Aries	Short stature, quiet voice, father a strong influence for good or ill. Possible military or paramilitary background.
Taurus	Bulldog appearance, materialistic parents—perhaps too much emphasis on keeping the furniture clean and not enough love.
Gemini	Clever and quick but not happy at school or at home. Orphaned, abandoned, or not wanted.
Cancer	Round face, good homemaker; close to mother or mother a powerful and scary figure.
Leo	Tall and nice-looking. A wanted child, but parents might have expected too much.
Virgo	Good-looking. Neglectful, difficult, or nutty mother. Much criticism in childhood; the person becomes critical later.
Libra	Very nice-looking. An easy childhood, but possibly given toys instead of attention. Absent or uninterested father.
Scorpio	Plain-looking. Mother loved the child but father was unavailable. Some feelings of not fitting in during early years.
Sagittarius	Long face. Little physical affection. Mother might be weak or nutty. Emphasis on religion and culture, which is later rejected.
Capricorn	Good bone structure. Hardship in the family, although the child is well loved. Learns early to save money and be cautious.
Aquarius	Very good-looking. Slightly off-the-wall parents. Emphasis on education, culture, and knowledge. Happy childhood, usually.
Pisces	Pasty face. Loneliness in childhood, possibly due to unfortunate circumstances. Artistic, athletic, or musical from an early age.

22

Finding Other Things in a Chart

We all know the sign that the Sun was in when we were born, because the Earth orbits the Sun in a regular pattern each year. The only discrepancy is likely to occur to those who were born on the cusp of two signs, but the question of which sign "rules" your Sun is easily answered by looking at your full birth chart, which can easily be obtained via the Internet, or links on my Web site at www.sashafenton.com.

This book has now shown you how to find the house that the Sun occupied when you born. We can even make a reasonable stab at working out the rising sign by the Sun's position on the time chart. However, there are factors that can make this position inaccurate, so it is better to get a chart made up properly, and a list of placements for the ascendant and the planets. Computers don't forget such things as daylight saving or British summer time, and they allow for the way the Sun appears to move over the surface of the earth at different times of the year.

When it comes to plotting the Moon's position, the situation is different. There are approximate moon-finder guides; I have used them in some of my books but they are not absolutely accurate, so once again, it is worth having a chart and a list of planetary positions made up. The Moon is interesting because it shows the hidden side of the personality and it gives the astrologer an opportunity to take a look at what someone really wants out of life.

Read *Your Secret Moon* by Anne Christie if you want to know more about the Moon.

Take a look at the Moon signs and houses in the celebrity charts in chapter 23. For instance, Nicholas Cage's Moon is in the cardinal sign of Libra and in the tenth house. Nicholas may be charming, but his inner nature forces him to consider his own needs and to have his own way. It also shows his ambition and drive. Even if his acting career faded, he would soon find another route upward. For one thing, the Moon looks for financial security when it is in the tenth house.

Consider Monica Lewinsky, whose Taurean Moon in the seventh house sends her looking for love and partnerships with smooth and charming men. Both Taurus and the seventh house are ruled by Venus, the planet of love, sophistication, luxury, status, and possessions. She may always go after men who seem to have it all, rather than find all of it for herself.

The remaining planets are not hard to understand either. Mercury rules various things, but above all, the person's mentality. Do you want your friends and lovers to have a practical turn of mind or do you prefer to be among those whose thinking is a little "off the wall?" Practicality is shown by the earth signs, ideas by the air signs, action by the fire signs, and emotion by the water signs. Consider how your mind works and how you want your associates to think, and look at Mercury.

Looking for love? Searching for sex? Try Venus and Mars. Both of these are sexy planets, although Venus represents feminine wiles and Mars is—in the words of one of our celebrities—the planet for, "a little more action and a little less conversation!"

Jupiter brings opportunities for expansion. This is hard to quantify, but it can mean expansion of your knowledge and gaining qualifications through further or higher education. This allows you to do more and be more than a basic education would. If you can teach, Jupiter will encourage that quality. Jupiter may take you traveling and expand your horizons, or it may encourage you to move to a larger house or expand your business—especially if the business includes an overseas or travel factor. Jupiter encourages spirituality, philosophy, religion, and the search for a belief—thus it expands the spiritual horizons.

Saturn is the planet of limitations, boundaries, and karma. New astrologers all hate Saturn and have conversations with each other about how bad it is to have Saturn in whatever sign and house theirs is. We all have a Saturn somewhere, so we might as well get used to it. At least it helps us to put down decent foundations and to finish what we start. We may find ourselves in hard situations at times, but Saturn gives us the endurance to make it through them.

Uranus is almost the opposite of Saturn, as it breaks down barriers. An astrologer friend of mine who has Aquarius rising (Uranus rules Aquarius) used to call this "the breakout planet." It can cause one to break out of past habits and lifestyles.

Neptune is the planet of psychism, dreams, escape, and sometimes revelation. It rules our interest in things that are hidden, thus in mystery and psychic matters. It also attracts us to art, music, and other things that bring us joy. We cannot see what is underwater unless we make an effort to go underwater too, and Neptune also rules the waves.

Pluto is a slow-moving planet that changes people's lives. It rarely does this overnight, even if the inciting event that forces the change seems to happen overnight; when one considers the situation, it is clear that it has been coming for some time. It also takes time for things to fall into a new pattern, for the state of upheaval to subside, and for people to come to terms with the changes that have occurred.

Chiron is a planetoid that was discovered in the 1970s. It relates to emotional hurt and sometimes to physical illness and injury. Depending on what other planets are involved in a Chiron transit, it can use illness or depression to encourage people to change direction in life. Chiron was a centaur who taught martial arts, music, and medicine, so it can also relate to learning about these things.

Here is a quick rundown of the planets and the signs with which they are associated, so if you want to look at the charts in this book in more detail, you can do so.

PLANET	SIGN	INTERPRETATION
Sun	Leo	Basic personality, love of music, charisma (if any)
Moon	Cancer	Mother, home, family, inner needs, emotional nature
Mercury	Gemini & Virgo	Mentality, siblings, local travel, communications, health matters
Venus	Taurus & Libra	Love, personal wealth and possessions, talent for creating beauty, music, partners, enemies
Mars	Aries	Activity, assertion, drive, battles
Jupiter	Sagittarius	Expansion, higher education, spirituality, philosophy, travel, legal matters, honesty
Saturn	Capricorn	Parents, especially the father, authority figures, ambition, hard work, attention to detail
Uranus	Aquarius	Originality, unconventionality, rebelliousness
Neptune	Pisces	Dreaminess, mysticism, artistic and musical creativity, self-undoing
Pluto	Scorpio	Power, sex, birth, death, shared resources, shared wealth, other people's money, hidden desires, hidden resentments

23

Examples

This chapter is full of birth charts, but don't let that frighten you, because all you need to look for at this stage is the symbol for the Sun—which is a circle with a dot inside it. Then look at the ascendant, which is at the nine o'clock position on the left-hand side of the chart. Finally, you can look for the symbol for the Moon. Unsurprisingly, this looks exactly like a new Moon.

The Moon sign and house represent the hidden, emotional side of a person. On the face of things, the Moon relates to home, family, and emotional matters, but it can reveal inner needs. In the kind of person who doesn't look too deeply into himself, the Moon's sign and house effect may be so well hidden that he may not really be aware of his own inner desires. At the end of this chapter, I will give you a very brief rundown of all the other planets so that you have the option of checking them out later if you want to—or of ignoring them if you don't.

First-House Sun

Nicholas Cage

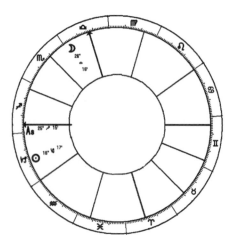

Nicholas Cage has Sagittarius rising, but his Sun is in Capricorn in the first house. Nicholas knows the value of hard work and of money, but he knows what his own talents are worth as well. With this placement, he must work hard to keep his body in good shape. The cool, friendly, detached, and self-possessed Nicholas has his Moon in the eleventh house in the sign of Libra.

Nicholas's strong body and his long face and long chin are typical of his Sagittarian rising sign, but his actual ascendant is toward the end of the Sagittarius, so most of his first house is occupied by Capricorn. Remember, the first house rules the body and often the appearance. Capricorn gives small rather than large lips and a smile where the corners of the mouth turn down. The Sun here emphasizes the Capricorn side of Nicholas's personality even more, but it also makes him lucky and successful, because it is easy to be a winner when the Sun is in the first house.

The tenth house is rather like Capricorn, so while Nicholas's Moon is in the sign of Libra, it is in this powerfully ambitious area of his chart. This placement often relates to writing ability, so perhaps one day Nicholas will write a bestseller.

Paul Newman

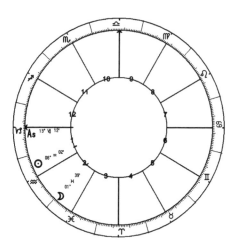

This is another cool character. He has the hardworking sign of Capricorn rising, and this speaks volumes about a tough childhood and parents who worked hard to become what they were. His first-house Sun is in Aquarius, but his Moon is in the emotionally vulnerable sign of Pisces in the materialistic and beauty-loving second house. What a complex character this is!

Aquarius is a charismatic sign, but when the Sun is in this sign in the first house, the charisma is emphasized. Capricorn rising suggests that Paul's outer manner and his approach to life are practical, and this is a good balance for the occasional silliness of a solar Aquarian. The combination of these two powerful signs being so prominent on his chart, along with the Sun in the first house make Paul the archetypal Aquarian "super-cool dude," and this placement also gives him his great smile. No wonder Paul gave a generation of film-going women the shivers!

Pisces rules film and photography, so whatever other ambitions Paul might have harbored, the Moon in his second house would have drawn him back to film work—although not necessarily as an actor.

Second-House Sun

Elvis Presley

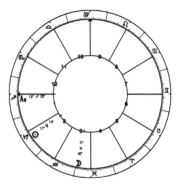

As we all know, Elvis Presley grew up in poverty and his real loves were his family and his music. His Sun in Capricorn made him work hard in order to dig his way out of his poor background. The fact that the Sun was in his second house shows his love of music and his desire to gain money and possessions—then the Sagittarian ascendant made him give most of his money away! This split in his personality makes him hard to understand. The Sagittarian ascendant gave Elvis a religious background that he alternately drew strength from and rejected. Elvis's Moon was in the third house, in the artistic, music-loving, creative, and emotionally vulnerable sign of Pisces.

The Sun in Capricorn in the second house should have made Elvis more cautious and businesslike than he was. It certainly helped to make him rich. Capricorn rules fathers and authoritative father figures, so he probably put too much trust in the mysterious "colonel" who took it upon himself to look after Elvis's affairs for him. Two mutable signs, Sagittarius rising and the Moon in Pisces, made it hard for Elvis to keep a grip on reality at times, or for him to understand what his own needs and feelings were. He must have needed to escape from reality at the end.

Lily Tomlin

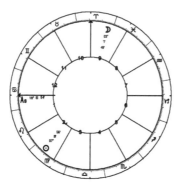

I don't know anything about Lily Tomlin's private life and personal circumstances, but her Sun in Virgo shows us that she has good powers of concentration, while the second-house position shows us that she focuses on both her image and her job. Her Cancer ascendant makes her a family person who probably saw her mother as a strong role model. This combination also shows us that Lily has striven hard to save money and she has probably invested it in property, land, or other shrewd ways. Her Moon sign is completely different, as it is spiritual rather than materialistic, and it shows a need to stretch her mind and to obtain space for personal andemotional freedom. Oddly enough, this Cancer-Virgo-Sagittarius mixture is not uncommon among actresses, because they are able to portray one personality while actually being something else underneath.

The Sun in the second house suggests that Lily likes material things and that she has a nice home and garden. Lily's Moon is in Aries, so despite her feminine looks—which derive from the feminine Cancer rising and equally feminine Sun in Virgo—she has a powerfully masculine inner drive.

Third-House Sun

Rupert Murdoch

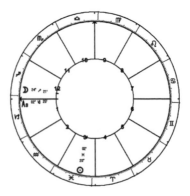

Rupert started with next to nothing and now he owns most of the world's media. His Capricorn ascendant attests to his lack of money and opportunities when young and to his ambition. His Sun is in the third house, of communications and journalism, but it is in the intuitive sign of Pisces. Rupert was born just before midnight, so although I am sure he would never reveal it, with the Sun in Pisces close to the bottom of the chart, Rupert must be a red-hot psychic! Even Rupert's Moon shrieks psychism, as it is in the intuitive twelfth house in Sagittarius. Could these factors have helped him to attain the peaks of business success?

Isn't it interesting that what we are taught to think of as the weak and dreamy sign of Pisces is shared by so many captains and kings of politics and industry, including both Vladimir Putin and Arial Sharon! Rupert's Piscean Sun is in the house that rules newspapers, and his Moon is in the idealistic sign of Sagittarius, but in the house of "politics"—the twelfth.

Neil Armstrong

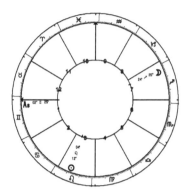

Interestingly, Neil Armstrong's Sun is also in the third house, in Leo. This rules local travel. Does an astronaut consider the Moon local? Perhaps he only thinks that distant travel starts at Alpha Centauri! Odder still is the Gemini rising sign, because Gemini also rules local travel. Neil's Moon says more about his lunar ambitions though, because it is in Sagittarius, and in the seventh house. Perhaps he was encouraged (or talked into) going to the Moon by others to some extent?

What would an astrologer expect to find on the chart of a pioneer of this quality? I would expect to find the Sun, Moon, or ascendant in Aries, a well-populated tenth house, and the signs of Sagittarius and Aquarius well in attendance. Neil's chart shows the Moon in adventurous Sagittarius but in the seventh house. Old-time astrologers assigned the father to the sign of Leo, so perhaps someone in a position of authority acted as a kind of father figure and thus encouraged him or gave him the opportunity.

Fourth-House Sun

Woody Allen

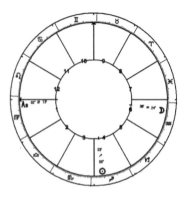

Woody Allen's mother and his Jewish family background are bound to have influenced him beneficially (and otherwise), so in his case, a fourth-house Sun makes sense. The Virgo ascendant tells us that Woody is meticulous, hardworking, and sometimes short of self-confidence. It is interesting to see how the issues of mothers and motherhood have worked their way out in his life, bearing in mind the scandal that arose when he ran off with his adopted daughter. Woody's Moon is in eccentric Sagittarius, which is a common situation among actors. It is also common among those who are born into one religious tradition but live differently once they become adults.

The ascendant often rules the outer appearance and manner, so Woody looks for all the world like a mousy, neurotic Virgo, and this is emphasized by his sixth-house Moon. He may be a hypochondriac or a worrier, and he certainly seems to be a perfectionist, but while he has done well as an actor, his fourth-house Sun shows that he is happiest when working behind the scenes.

Prince Charles

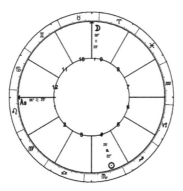

If the Sun in the fourth house represents a powerful mother and an attachment to family heritage, Britain's Prince Charles's chart says it all. The Prince's Sun in Scorpio suggests that he carries a bag of resentment around with him—doing his duty, but frequently resenting the situation into which he was born. It seems that the heir to the British throne has always felt restricted by his status. The Moon sits right at the top of the chart, once again showing how his mother's attitudes and his family heritage rule him. The ascendant in the "royal" sign of Leo denotes that he was born into this situation and that only the strangest of circumstances are likely to release him from it. Just as Cancer and the Moon rule the mother, so Leo and the Sun are said by some older astrological traditions to rule the father—and Charles's father is also royal, both by his marriage to Queen Elizabeth and by birth.

As a Scorpio with the Sun in the fourth house, Prince Charles is home-loving and patriotic. This placement often goes with shyness, so he must have had to learn to cope with all the public relations work that he does. The combination of Scorpio and the fourth house would have fitted him for a naval career, so it is a shame that he has not been able to fulfill that side of his nature.

Fifth-House Sun

Oprah Winfrey

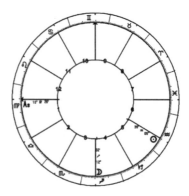

Outgoing Oprah has her Sun in the fifth house, which is very common in the entertainment business. She brings fun into many people's lives in an original and inimitable style, which is right for an Aquarian. She helps humanity and she does it all via the medium of television rather than face-to-face. Oprah's rising sign is Virgo, which talks of a difficult childhood and tough circumstances. Like so many people who broadcast and who spread ideals around, her Moon is in Sagittarius. It is also in the fourth house, so she is also very close to her parents and other relatives, and she protects them from public scrutiny.

Oprah's charisma and good looks are typical of her Aquarian Sun in the fifth house. The Virgo ascendant and Sagittarian Moon give her an interest in psychology and in people, so she has married her talents together in an exceptionally successful manner. Her Moon is down on the IC (the immum coeli, or the nadir), which shows that she respects her mother and the family, and the background that did so much to shape her. She keeps her private life away from the public gaze.

Hillary Clinton

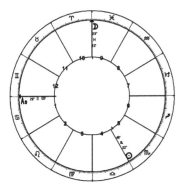

Hillary Clinton's fifth house suggests that she is close to her daughter, Chelsea, and that she may have centered her life on her when she was young, but it can also indicate that she loves her husband, despite his faults. Scorpios carry a certain amount of resentment around with them, and Hillary is probably no exception. Her Gemini ascendant signifies that she did not receive sufficient emotional nurturing during childhood. Her Moon is in the compassionate sign of Pisces, but it is at the top of the chart, so it seems that her mother expected a great deal of her and that Hillary now expects a great deal of herself. Will she become president one day? Possibly, but vice president is more likely, as Scorpios are often more comfortable in the number two position.

Notice how Hillary's Sun, Moon, and ascendant are all on the cusp of two signs and two houses. This gives Hillary the ability to switch from one thing to another far more easily than her Scorpio Sun would suggest. We don't see this side of her, but it looks as though she might be moody and apt to change her mind or change direction when her mood changes.

Sixth-House Sun

Martin Sheen

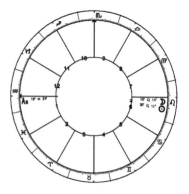

Martin's glamour comes from his Sun and Moon in Leo, but both are in the meticulous and hardworking sixth house. I bet that Martin has turned down many party invitations so that he could spend time learning his lines and rehearsing. His rising sign is Aquarius, so he really is as liberal and humanitarian as he appears to be in *The West Wing*. He has even campaigned against the war in Iraq! This rising sign also adds to his considerable charisma and gives him his wonderful gaze.

What could be more glamorous and charismatic than Martin's Sun and Moon conjunction in Leo and his Aquarian ascendant? However, the sixth house makes him more likely to want to serve in some way than to be a leader, so he is right to play the part of president than to try to be one—although we all suspect that with a good spin doctor writing great lines for him, he would do a wonderful job. Bring on Jeb Bartlett!

Steven Spielberg

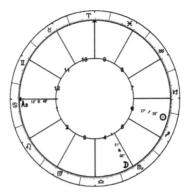

Steven also has his Sun in the sixth house in the sign of Sagittarius, so his religious background has obviously influenced his politics, ideals, and ideas. This also makes him an original thinker, but one who is able to cope with the vast number of details that filmmaking entails. Steven's ascendant is in Cancer, and the film that brought him to prominence (*ET*) was all about a lost child (ET) wanting to get back to his mom and his family. Steven's Moon is in the fourth house in Scorpio, and this adds to his sense of history and possibly to his determination to fight anti-Semitism and a recurrence of the Holocaust.

Steven's Sagittarian Sun gives him the artistry and imagination to make his wonderful films, while the sixth-house position ensures that he focuses on good scripts. His films appeal to families, so going to one of them is often a family affair. This makes sense when one considers his Cancer ascendant.

Seventh-House Sun

Robert Kennedy

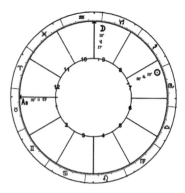

Robert's Sun was in the seventh house in Scorpio. Every sign and house has good and bad things attached to it, but Robert seems to have found all the downsides to his combination. The seventh house is associated with love and partnership, but also with open enemies. Scorpio is associated with commitment but also with hidden enemies—and with death, among other things. This sign and house combination is also an intensely sexy one. Scorpio is associated with family wealth and wealthy partners and colleagues, while his Taurus rising sign refers to his own personal wealth. He could probably have lived a life of ease without working at all, but his hardworking Capricorn Moon at the top of his chart wouldn't have allowed that. His greatest partnership was probably with his brother, but his Moon shows that he harbored secret dreams of following John Kennedy into the top job at the White House one day; it is quite possible that he might have achieved this goal had he not been assassinated.

Princess Diana

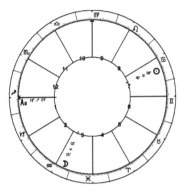

A seventh-house Sun is not necessarily a recipe for tragedy, but like Robert Kennedy's, it contains the seeds of sadness and loss. We all know Diana's story well, so there is no need to repeat it here. Her Cancer Sun in the seventh house made her a wonderful mother figure, a lovely-looking woman, and pleasant person, but the cardinal and angular combination shows that she liked having her own way. Her Sagittarian ascendant drew her into spiritual matters, but it also gave her a longing for freedom and independence, along with her somewhat cool and detached Aquarian Moon. A Moon in the third house shows an attachment to brothers and sisters, but not much love coming from parents, lovers, and partners.

A combination of the Sun in Cancer and Sagittarius rising would have made Princess Diana a wonderful teacher. It is interesting to note that before her marriage to Prince Charles, she worked as a nursery attendant and teacher. The Moon in the slightly revolutionary sign of Aquarius and the communicative third house show that Princess Diana knew how to use the media to full advantage.

Eighth-House Sun

John F. Kennedy

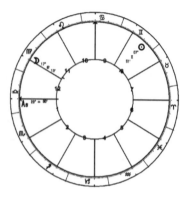

It is almost inevitable that President Kennedy would have his Sun in the sexy eighth house, but the sheer number of planets in the house of sex and death is not a good sign. His Gemini Sun indicates a quick and clever brain. His Libra ascendant gave him his charisma, attractive personality, charm, and good looks. John Kennedy's Moon was in the highly intelligent and diligent sign of Virgo, and it was in the equally intelligent eleventh house. He must have been wonderful company.

Libra on the ascendant is notoriously flirtatious. President Clinton also had Libra rising. Sex is for fun for these people and it may represent a way of relaxing and leaving behind the cares and worries that accompany such a high-powered job. Cancer at the top of John Kennedy's chart shows that the public loved him, whatever he did. However, the collection of badly placed planets not shown here suggests the tragedy that eventually befell him.

Sean Connery

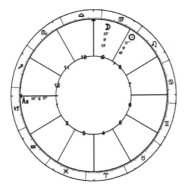

Sean also has his Sun in the charismatic eighth house; as far as I know, he is not a womanizer, but British *People* magazine voted him the "Sexiest Man Alive" in 1989. Oddly enough, before he was married he had an affair with one of Marilyn Monroe's roommates and perhaps with Marilyn as well, which gives him a strange connection with John Kennedy. Sean Connery came to prominence through his role as James Bond, so the first time that most of us saw of him, he was holding a pistol in that famous opening shot. This image is typical of an eighth-house Sun, but his modest, hardworking Virgo Sun and Moon and his quietly ambitious Capricorn ascendant are closer to reality. It is interesting that Sean really made his way in a foreign country, as his ninth-house Moon indicates.

An eighth-house Sun shows that money, possessions, resources, and other things that have to be shared with others, that come via others, or that are administered by others can be a problem. In Sean's case, he had very little money as a young man and this affected his mind-set. This, along with his careful Virgo Sun and skinflint Capricorn ascendant, make him the notorious miser that he is reputed to be.

Ninth-House Sun

Al Gore

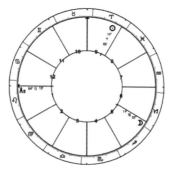

Al nearly made it, didn't he? Well, let's not get into that debate, but it is interesting to note that like George W. Bush, Al Gore has Leo rising. His Sun is in the "political" sign of Aries, but it is in the ninth house, of travel and education, so he must have had a better handle on foreign affairs than President Bush. Al's Moon is in the fifth house, which suggests that he cares deeply for his children and he knows how to relax and have fun, but it is also in the ambitious and hardworking sign of Capricorn.

The Moon in Capricorn suggests that Al may have been pushed by his parents and other authority figures to become a great achiever, and the Leo ascendant ratifies this. The Sun in Aries makes him willing and able to accept command of his country, but the ninth house is a little too idealistic and lacking in raw ambition for him to push hard enough to get there.

Severiano Ballesteros

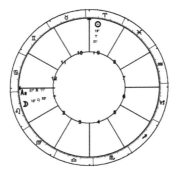

For those who are not familiar with golf, Steve is a champion Spanish golfer and the first of a number of Spaniards who have become famous for their golfing achievements. His Cancer ascendant makes him pleasant and personable, while his ninth-house Sun has taken him traveling around the world. It also made him internationally famous. It is interesting to see that the Sun is at the top of the chart, which symbolizes a person who strives to reach the top. His Sun is in Aries, which is often a sign of athletic ability. Seve's Moon is in the first house in Leo, so he must have been dedicated to making a success of himself from an early age. The Leo and Cancer connection suggests that his parents helped him achieve his ambitions.

The ninth house is associated with sports, while Aries tends to like handling tools, bats, racquets, and so on. This combination has helped Seve to become a great golfer, but if he had decided on badminton, tennis, cricket, baseball, or any other bat-and-ball sport, he would have been equally successful.

Tenth-House Sun

Monica Lewinsky

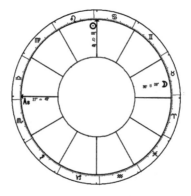

Monica's Sun is at the top of the chart in the tenth house, so she is ambitious and determined, and it is possible that her father influenced her. This placement denotes help (or otherwise) from people in positions of authority, but it can also lead to a very public downfall. However, her Sun is to the right of the letters MC (the midheaven) and this makes her something of a risk taker. Her Leo Sun denotes pride, so perhaps she will make a fresh start somewhere. Her Libra ascendant shows charm and charisma, but while it makes her ambitious, it asks others to help her to get where she wants to be. Coupled with her Taurus Moon and seventh-house Leo Sun, this ascendant can make her lazy.

Nobody can feel love more deeply than the signs of Cancer and Leo, and Monica's Sun is on the cusp of these signs, incorporating the energies of both. Libra suggests an attraction to (and for) people who are much older or much younger than oneself.

Mia Farrow

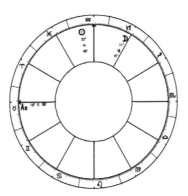

Mia Farrow was an actress in her own right and a one-time girlfriend of Frank Sinatra before she married Woody Allen; she then adopted several children. It seems that Mia is ambitious but in a strange way, because her Sun is in the unconventional sign of Aquarius. Her Taurus ascendant suggests common sense, as does her Moon in Capricorn, while her Aquarian Sun craves space. She could be happy with her detached relationship and being away from the public gaze.

The combination of the Sun in Aquarius at the top of the chart and the Moon in the idealistic ninth house, in sensible but ambitious Capricorn, could make Mia a wonderful force for change in the world. It is very likely that she has done more than her share of fund-raising for needy children and others.

Eleventh-House Sun

Cher

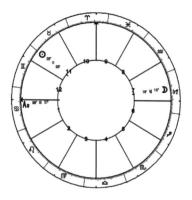

Cher's Sun in the eleventh house symbolizes her eccentricity and originality. Being in Taurus, it is associated with music and especially with singing. Taureans are often "dressy" and a bit over the top, and the eleventh house is always unconventional, so this fits. Her Cancer ascendant shows her fondness for family life and the influence that her actress mother had on her. Her Capricorn Moon tells us that she looks after her relatives (probably all of them) very well. Her Moon is in the seventh house, which is also associated with music and with love, but this can bring emotional domination by others, as appeared to happen when she was with Sonny Bono.

This may sound strange, but I bet Cher is a wonderful cook. If she ever needed to look for a different career, she could open a chain of wonderful restaurants—and just imagine the decor!

Michael Douglas

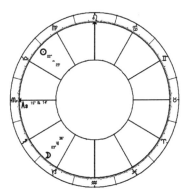

Michael's sexy Libran Sun is in the friendly eleventh house. As it happens, Catherine Zeta-Jones is also a Libran, so they should get along well together. His Scorpio ascendant adds to his amazingly sexy charisma, but his Capricorn Moon shows less self-confidence on the inside than one might imagine. The Moon is in the second house, so my guess is that he works hard to keep his good image, looks, and charisma. The Capricorn Moon also suggests that—perhaps unwittingly—he has made an effort to follow his father's example.

The popular press jokes about the age gap between Michael Douglas and his wife, Catherine Zeta-Jones. Tradition says that the Moon in Capricorn makes a person interested in older partners, but I have found that it just instigates an age difference that can go in either direction. Libra is another sign that likes age differences, so the age gap suits this couple.

Twelfth-House Sun

Tony Blair

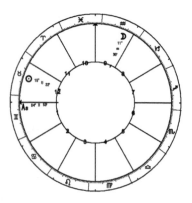

Tony's twelfth-house Sun in Taurus suggests a mixture of practicality and idealism, but also great strategic ability and the ability to hang in there when the going gets tough. His Gemini ascendant symbolizes his amazing ability to communicate and to persuade—and his boyish looks. Tony's Moon is in the idealistic sign of Aquarius and in the eleventh house, so this shows a certain detachment and little need to spend much time with his family, but a strong attachment and much loyalty toward his friends.

Tony Blair's Sun is in the twelfth house. The same goes for the British chancellor of the exchequer, Gordon Brown, and the British home secretary, David Blunkett, as well as George Bush, John Kerry, Arial Sharon, Vladimir Putin, and allegedly, the late Yassir Arafat. This placement seems to be a common signature for leaders and wannabe leaders.

Madonna

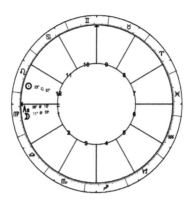

Madonna's Leo Sun symbolizes her desire to be in the field of entertainment, but that is about all that is obvious about her. The twelfth-house placement shows the amount of thought that she puts into her work, while her Virgo Moon in the first house shows her determination to succeed through hard work. This Moon also denotes deep feelings that she keeps to herself. Her Virgo ascendant suggests that she had a tough childhood and that she may never have been able to please her parents. A sunrise Virgo Moon shows that she may have had a critical and disapproving mother, or one who was not quite sane.

Does Madonna want to become a world leader? Her nervy Virgo Moon would make it hard for her to do so, but she is certainly the leading figure in her branch of show business. It will be interesting to see how she handles her children and the press as time goes by.

And Finally ...

Ronnie and Reggie Kray

Here are two names that people outside Great Britain and even younger Brits may not recognize, but older Britons will definitely know who they are. These are the notorious Kray twins, who terrorized London's gangland in the 1960s.

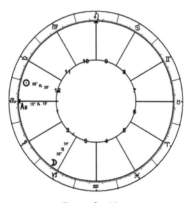

Ronnie Kray

They eventually spent much of their lives locked away—Reggie in prison and Ronnie in a secure mental hospital. Look at the charismatic and dangerous Scorpio Suns and ascendants, but the Suns are in the twelfth house, indicating long-term incarceration. They were extremely good to their parents and very close to their

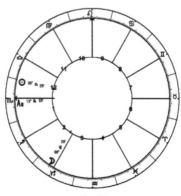

Reggie Kray

loving mother—as shown by their Moons in Capricorn—while the third-house connection suggests that they were also very close to each other.

Let's Take This One Step Further

Mercury rising in Scorpio makes for quick, intelligent minds and good heads for business. Mars in the first house is a signature of aggression, so the Mercury-Mars combination would indicate both physical and verbal aggression. Mars in Sagittarius in the first house tells us that they were both sexual predators and possibly also sexual sadists. It is interesting that Ronnie has both Mars and Venus in conjunction in the same house, while Reggie does not. Ronnie was gay—not an easy thing to be in the early 1960s and in gangland to boot!

Saturn in the third house at the bottom of the chart shows that their eventual forced parting from each other and from their family must have been painful for them, and this pain endured for a long period. Uranus in the sixth house suggests that they took an odd attitude to their "work" and, being in Aries, it shows an aggressively odd attitude at that. Pluto in the ninth house in Cancer is in a T-square aspect to the Sun in Scorpio and Uranus in Aries, making their fame for being close to their family and for dealing in death an international matter. The trine from Pluto to Mercury suggests that they were happy for others to know about their power and to fear it. The square between Pluto and the Sun is dangerous, though, and if the Suns had been in any other house than the twelfth, someone would have killed them, sooner or later.

Neptune in the tenth house in Virgo is something of an Achilles heel, as verbal Virgo suggests that someone spoke out of turn and betrayed them—thus ending their (tenth-house) career. Neptune is badly aspected to both Mars and Venus, so open enemies must have helped in their downfall. Jupiter in the eleventh house in Libra indicates that they had many influential friends who helped them earn great sums of money, but these friends must also have helped them spend it.

The dangerous twelfth-house Suns are in opposition to Uranus, suggesting a sudden turn of events against them. However, Jupiter and Saturn in a trine aspect suggest that their family never abandoned them. The Mars-Jupiter sextile is lucky, but Reggie has a Venus-Sun semisquare that Ronnie does not share. He must have been aware that Ronnie's increasing eccentricity and his homosexuality (at that time of nonacceptance) was damaging to their images. The Moon trines Neptune, allowing them to realize their dreams, but it also squares Jupiter and semisquares Mercury— so somehow they lacked knowledge and information about of things that were going on behind their backs. They kept much hidden from the world, but the world also kept much hidden from them—as shown by the twelfth-house Suns in Scorpio, and Mercury and the ascendant in Scorpio.

Index